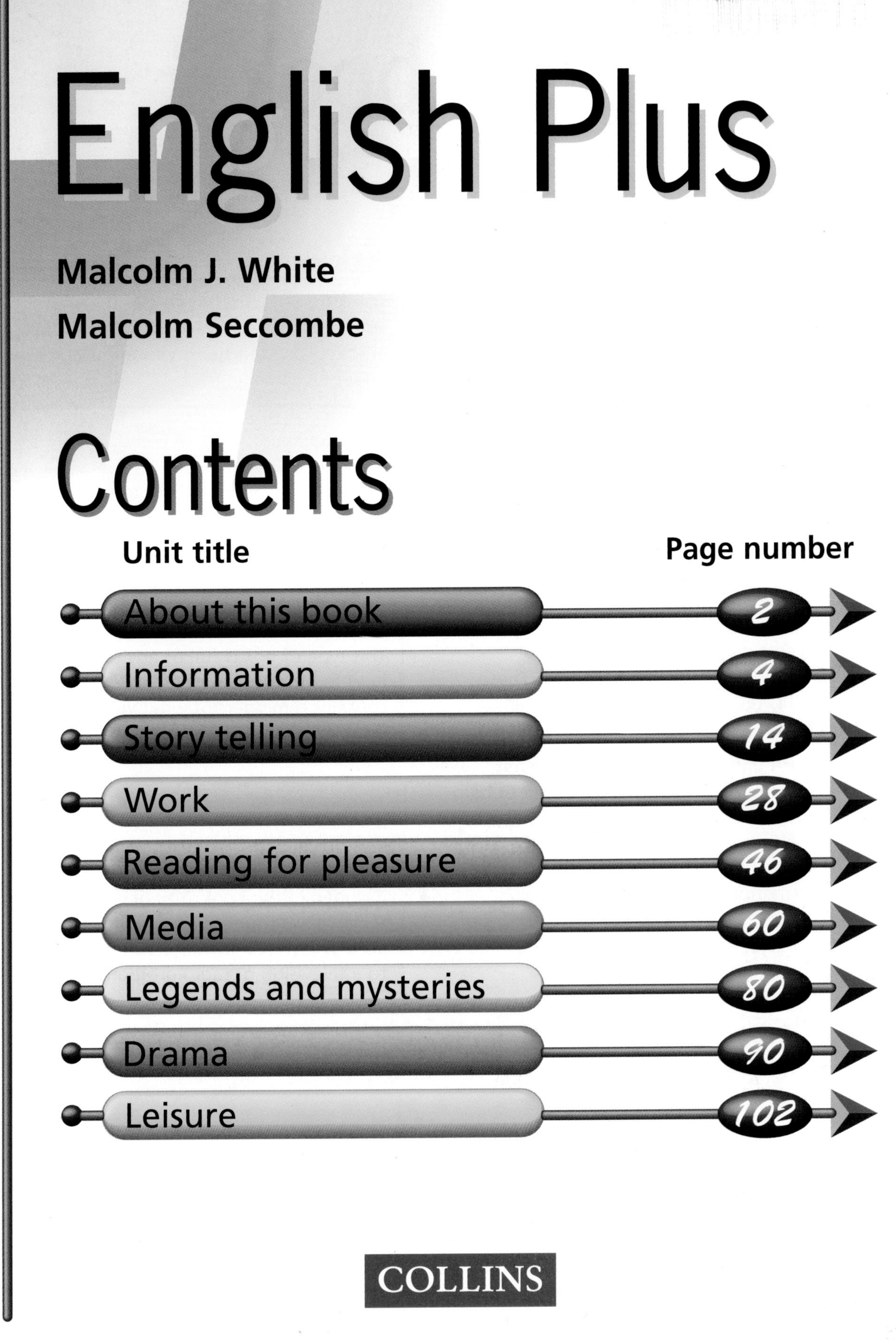

English Plus

Malcolm J. White

Malcolm Seccombe

Contents

COLLINS

About this book

To the student

This book has been written to help you to prepare for the Certificate of Achievement and GCSE qualifications. There are eight units to work through. Each of them is set out in exactly the same way. You will soon understand how the units are organised, which will help you to improve and succeed.

Each unit begins with a title page. This contains pictures which show many of the things you will be working on, together with a list of the work you will need to complete to achieve the unit in your final assessment. Your teacher may also give you a check-list of tasks you should complete to obtain your certificate. In some schools, students may receive certificates for successfully completing each unit. These certificates could be included in your National Record of Achievement folders.

In each unit there are some important boxes that have been colour-coded to help you. You will quickly get into the habit of using them as you work through the unit. Each box contains a particular type of information or advice.

Task

This kind of box tells you exactly what you have to do. Always read it carefully and ask your teacher if you are unsure about anything in it.

How?

These boxes contain advice about how to carry out the task you have been set. You will find these boxes very helpful.

Tips for success

This type of box is full of advice about how to produce your best work. It also contains reminders of what your teacher is looking for in your work.

Research

This box is used whenever you are asked to find some information that is not included in the book. You may be asked to talk to another person, go to a library, use a CD-ROM, or watch or listen to a television or radio programme.

To the teacher

We have written this book to cater for a number of your needs in preparing students for the Certificate of Achievement and GCSE qualifications. While the book's primary objective is to help students meet the requirements of the Certificate course, the content also allows students access to GCSE assessment criteria.

Our experience shows that working with self-contained units, as set out in this book, is a strong motivating factor, especially for students who respond well to short-term, highly structured goals. However, as the structure of the tasks is applicable to all levels of ability, the units may also be used to motivate those who require extra help to reach their full potential in their GCSE course, or as preparatory work for more able students. This makes the book particularly appropriate for use with mixed-ability teaching groups.

The way in which the units are organised enables students to:

- Acquire *knowledge*, *skills* and *understanding.*
- Apply their learning in a range of contexts.

The **Task**, **How?**, Tips for success and Research boxes have been colour-coded to help you and your students to identify clearly *requirements* and *advice* or *guidance*.

The Teacher's File that accompanies this student's book provides material and ideas both to support and extend students across the ability range. The templates included in the Teacher's File assist students in framing appropriate responses.

In addition to meeting the demands of the syllabus, we believe we have designed a course book that students will find stimulating, challenging and, most of all, fun to work with. In conjunction with the Teacher's File, we have also sought to provide you with a ready-made resource that enables you to get the best out of your students in ways that are both interesting and rigorous.

Finally, we believe that you will find that the materials provided can be used imaginatively and flexibly, especially if you are also using the support material in the Teacher's File. The important thing is that assessment objectives are met and that students understand what those objectives are.

Information

Objectives

In successfully completing this unit, you will:

1. Prepare a school visit to London.
2. Select a major event to visit.
3. Plan additional activities.
4. Present a timetable for the day.
5. Write a letter giving details of the visit to parents.

Introduction

In this unit, you are going to plan a trip to London for a group of students in your year. Your teacher has agreed to allow you to choose where you go from a list that she has provided. The main event will be just one part of the day. You have to plan the whole outing. This will include:

- Planning the transport.
- Selecting the main event.
- Providing a choice of activities to fill the rest of the day.
- Arranging a meal.
- Seeking the permission of parents.
- Presenting a complete plan.

Task

Look at the pictures on the previous page.

Discuss the types of activities they show.

How?

During your discussion, you might talk about:

A Activities that interest you.
B Activities that would be popular with people of your age-group.
C Activities that are not shown.
D The sort of trip to London in which you would be interested.

Tips for success

- Make sure you understand the tasks.
- Making notes before the discussion may help you to remember the things you want to talk about.
- Use the How? box to help you through the activity.
- Speak clearly.
- Explain carefully.
- Listen to others.
- Take turns.

Choosing an event

Task

Choose the main event for your trip from the following three options:

- The Millenium Theme Park.
- The Europa Cup Final.
- The Rage concert.

A Make a note of dates, times and costs.

B Your teacher will help you to make your choice.

C A planning worksheet may be available to help you.

The Millenium Theme Park

The ultimate in 21st-century fun!

Open daily April to October
10.00 a.m. to 10.00 p.m.
Just 3 miles off the M1

Admission
Adults £10
Children £7.50
Coach parties welcome

Ride 'The Hurricane'

... if you dare!

Tips for success

- Discuss your choice with at least one other person.
- Choose the event you think will be enjoyed by most people.

The Amateur Athletics Association presents the

Europa Cup Final

Britain's male and female athletes take on the best of Europe on British soil.

Who will be crowned champions of Europe?

France
Germany
Italy
Russia
Spain
United Kingdom

July 16th
7.00 p.m to 10.00 p.m.
Tickets
Adults £15.00
Children £7.00

The Rage

Manic Energy Tour

with supporting artists

London Arena
July 16th, 17th, 18th
at 6.45 p.m.

Tickets from the box office
£7.00, £10.00, £15.00, £22.00

Travel

To make the most of your trip, it has been agreed that you will aim to arrive in London before mid-day and be home around midnight.

The first stage of your journey involves catching a local bus from Hampton, where you live, to Middlewick Station. Here you will catch the Intercity train to Euston Station, London.

Task

Use the bus and train timetables provided to plan the times and the cost of your transport arrangements.

How?

- **A** Choose a train that will arrive in London before midday.
- **B** Make a note of the time it leaves Middlewick.
- **C** Choose a bus that arrives in Middlewick in time for you to catch the train.
- **D** Make a note of the time the bus leaves Hampton.
- **E** Work out how much the train tickets and the bus tickets will cost for each person.
- **F** If you have one, complete the transport section of your planning worksheet.

Tips for success

- Take care reading the timetables.
- Remember that bus and train timetables use the 24-hour clock.

Melchester → London Euston

Melchester	07.20	08.20	08.30	09.20	10.20
Stoke	08.01	09.01	–	10.01	11.01
Middlewick	08.47	09.47	–	10.47	11.47
Milton Keynes	08.52	09.52	09.50	10.52	11.52
Watford Junction	09.17	10.17	–	11.17	11.52
London Euston	09.52	10.52	10.40	11.52	12.52

London Euston → Melchester

London Euston	20.00	21.00	22.00	22.30	00.00
Watford Junction	20.35	21.35	22.35	23.05	24.35
Milton Keynes	21.00	22.00	23.00	23.30	01.00
Middlewick	21.15	22.15	23.15	23.45	01.15
Stoke	21.51	22.51	23.51	01.21	01.51
Melchester	22.32	23.32	00.32	02.02	02.32

Fares Middlewick-Euston (return)

First class £74 Second class £34
Saver Plus £26 Students £17
Party rates (for a group of ten or more, aged 17 and under) £13

Service 152 Trentham to Middlewick

Trentham	08.00	08.30	09.00	10.00	11.00	12.00
Merton	08.10	08.40	09.10	10.10	11.10	12.10
Hampton	08.15	08.45	09.15	10.15	11.15	12.15
Birley Village	08.17	08.47	09.17	10.17	11.17	12.17
Dibley Grange	08.25	08.55	09.25.	10.25	11.25	12.25
Barnton Road	08.30	09.00	09.40	10.40	11.40	12.40
Middlewick Station	08.40	09.10	09.40	10.40	11.40	12.40

Service 152 Middlewick to Trentham

		*	*	*
Middlewick Station	22.30	*23.15*	*23.50*	*01.00*
Barnton Road	22.40	–	*00.00*	–
Dibley Grange	22.45	*23.30*	–	*01.15*
Birley Village	22.53	–	*23.40*	–
Hampton	22.55	*23.40*	*00.15*	*01.25*
Merton	23.00	–	*00.20*	–
Trentham	23.10	*23.55*	*00.30*	*01.40*

Fares

Hampton-Middlewick 55p **All-night bus – double fare*

Places to go

It has been agreed that you will have a packed lunch, but you will all meet later for a meal in a restaurant before going on to the main event. After eating your lunch, you will have about five hours to fill before you meet up again for your evening meal and go on to your main event. The time between lunch and the evening meal will be filled by visiting up to two places of interest in London.

Task

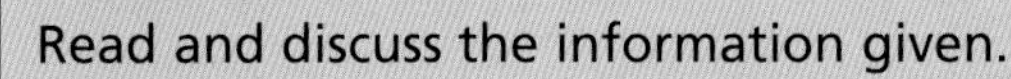

Read and discuss the information given.

Choose the two events or activities that you think would be most popular with people of your age.

Give reasons why they would be popular.

How?

A Look at all the possible choices very closely.

B By talking with someone else, put the choices in order of popularity among your age-group.

C With at least one other person, agree on your top two choices.

D If you have one, complete a planning chart.

Tips for success

- Make sure you understand the tasks.
- Making notes before the discussion may help you to remember the things you want to talk about.
- Use the How? box to help you through the activity.
- Speak clearly.
- Explain carefully.
- Listen to others.
- Take turns.
- Remember that you are planning for other people, not just for yourself.
- Try to avoid choosing two similar events.
- Think about cost.

Tower of London

St Paul's Cathedral

London Zoo

Imperial War Museum

Chessington World of Adventures

Camden Market

British Museum

MADAME TUSSAUD'S

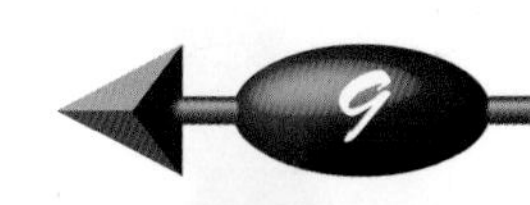

Eating out

For your evening meal, the restaurant has agreed to a special group rate of £10.00 per person, including a free soft drink.

Task

Read the menu provided by the restaurant.

Make up three menus to offer the group.

One must contain a FISH main course.

One must contain a MEAT main course.

One must be suitable for VEGETARIANS.

How?

- **A** Separate the main courses into FISH, MEAT and VEGETARIAN.
- **B** Decide which main course in each group would be the most popular.
- **C** Make a note of the price of the most popular main course in each group.
- **D** List the starters according to price.
- **E** List the desserts according to price.
- **F** Choose one starter and one dessert to complete each menu.
- **G** A menu worksheet might be available for you to complete.

Tips for success

- Make sure that all parts of the vegetarian menu are suitable for vegetarians.
- Make sure that your menus appeal to a range of tastes.
- Make sure that each menu costs no more than £10.00 per person.
- You could use a calculator to help work out the cost of each menu.

MENU

• Starters •

Spare ribs *£2.50*

French onion soup *£2.10*

Prawn cocktail *£2.75*

• Main Courses •

Vegetable lasagne with salad *£5.50*

Scampi with chips and peas *£4.75*

Hamburger in a bun with chips and salad *£4.75*

Sausages, mash and baked beans *£4.25*

Nut roast with potatoes and salad *£4.75*

Cod in batter with chips and peas *£5.50*

Spaghetti bolognese *£5.50*

Jacket potato with Tuna salad *£4.25*

• Desserts •

Apple crumble with custard *£3.00*

Chocolate, vanilla or strawberry ice cream *£2.25*

Fresh fruit salad *£2.80*

Black Forest gâteau *£3.00*

Enjoy your meal!

The plan

Now that you have finished your planning, you will need to set out all the details of the trip for the teacher in charge of the visit.

Task

Using the information you have gathered, you will now need to write down the arrangements for the whole day from the time you leave Hampton to the time you return.

How?

- **A** Give clear information.
- **B** Set out the information step-by-step in the order in which things will happen.
- **C** Give accurate timings to show how well-organised your trip is.

Tips for success

- Sort out your information clearly.
- Use a time-line.
- Be brief and accurate.

Selling the idea

Now that you have organised everything, there are two more things you need to do to make your visit a success:

- Persuade your year group to take part.
- Inform parents of your plans and seek their permission for their son or daughter to be involved.

Task

Design a poster advertising the trip for display around school.

How?

A Choose a design that will attract attention.
B Choose carefully the details that you will need to include.

Tips for success

- Make sure your design is appropriate for a trip to London.
- Think about how to get the main event you have chosen across to the people who will see the poster.
- Think about how to interest people of your age in the visit.
- Remember that the most effective posters are:
  Simple and colourful.
  Not too crowded.
  Written in a variety of print styles.
  Clear in what they say.
- Your poster should answer the following questions:
  Who is the trip for?
  What will the trip include?
  When is it going to take place?
  Where is it going?
  How much will it cost?

Writing to parents

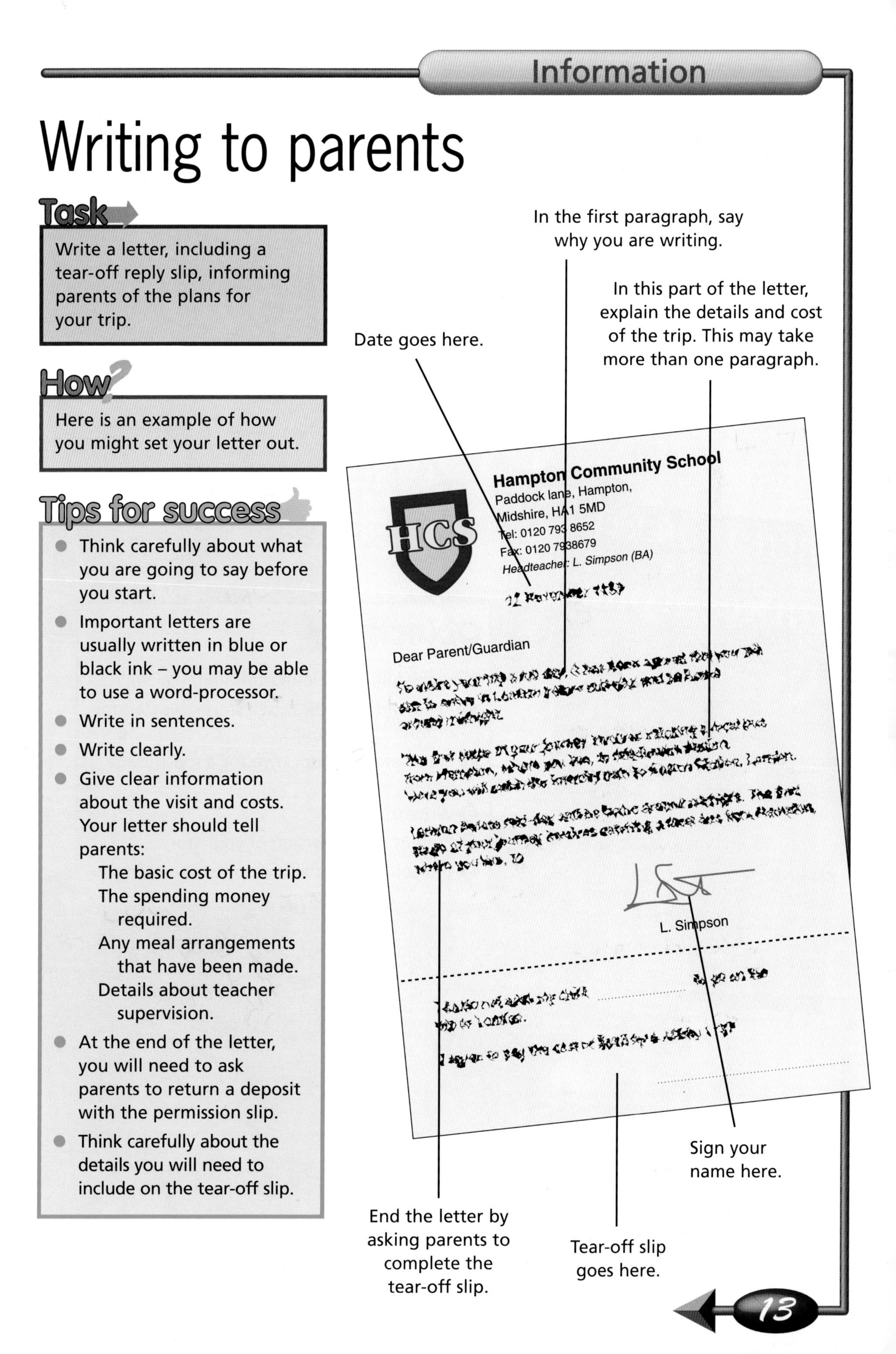

Task

Write a letter, including a tear-off reply slip, informing parents of the plans for your trip.

How?

Here is an example of how you might set your letter out.

Tips for success

- Think carefully about what you are going to say before you start.
- Important letters are usually written in blue or black ink – you may be able to use a word-processor.
- Write in sentences.
- Write clearly.
- Give clear information about the visit and costs. Your letter should tell parents:
  - The basic cost of the trip.
  - The spending money required.
  - Any meal arrangements that have been made.
  - Details about teacher supervision.
- At the end of the letter, you will need to ask parents to return a deposit with the permission slip.
- Think carefully about the details you will need to include on the tear-off slip.

Story telling

Objectives

In successfully completing this unit, you will:

1. Read and talk about two stories written for different age groups.
2. Plan a story of your own for a specific age group.
3. Write the story.
4. Present a final version of your story.
5. Tell your story to at least one other person.

Introduction

In this unit, you are going to read and talk about two stories written for children of different age groups. You then have to plan and write a story on your own.

Task

Look at the pictures on the previous page.

Discuss the types of stories they show, and the age groups that they are written for.

How?

During your discussion, talk about any differences you can find between the types of books shown in the picture. Look at:

A The sort of pictures used.
B The number of words used.
C The difficulty of the words used.
D The way the book covers are set out.

Tips for success

- Make sure you understand the tasks.
- Making notes before the discussion may help you to remember the things you want to talk about.
- Use the How? box to help you through the activity.
- Speak clearly.
- Explain carefully.
- Listen to others.

the Sleepover Club at Kenny's

FOR BOYS!

LYNNE REID BANKS

Harry the Poisonous Centipede

ILLUST...
TONY...

Jumbo Jets

We Won the Lottery

5 30 16 13 45 18

Shoo Rayner

Here is a story written by Tony when he was sixteen. It is about something that happened to him when he was thirteen.

Jason Jones

Even when I look back on it now, I still feel ashamed of what I did. There he was, curled up on the floor clutching his stomach, and begging me not to kick him again. His eyes flashed with fear as he pleaded for mercy. He was bleeding from the nose and his words were gulped out between sobs.

"Please, Tony, don't. I haven't done anything wrong."

"You have, you git, and you know it."

With that, my boot thudded into his ribs again and I heard him wince with pain before I turned quickly and ran.

Jason Jones ruined things when I was thirteen. Until then, Mark and I had been inseparable. They used to call us the terrible twins. We met on the first day at primary school and had been together ever since. We were brothers, not blood-related, but bonded together by our interests and our friendship.

In school we would stick up for each other and in class we had to be separated because we chatted so much. We were always looking for fun or a stunt that we could pull off together. Once we set an alarm clock to go off at 9.15 a.m. and hid it on top of the loudspeaker in the Assembly Hall. Mr Wailes, the headteacher, was droning on about being good citizens when the alarm bell rang out. Old Wailes went red with fury while the whole school erupted into laughter. I looked at Mark and he just winked. Afterwards, we laughed when we remembered the looks on the teachers' faces. We were buddies. Mates. Unbeatable.

Then, when we were twelve, we went on holiday together. My mum hired a cottage in Wales and we invited Mark to come with us. We spent long, glorious days swimming, fishing, and playing in the sand dunes. At night, we would sit outside and watch the tide roll in, discussing our plans for the future. We wanted to travel, to see the sights of the world. Our ambitions were limitless, but wherever we travelled, whoever we met, and however long we were separated, we would always be mates.

Then, one February morning, Jason Jones walked into our lives. He arrived during a Geography lesson. Mr Wailes opened the door to our classroom and marched in, trailing a thin, fair-haired boy behind him.

"This is Jason Jones," he announced. "He is new to the school, from Cardiff. I know you will make him welcome. Mark Thomas, you will show him the ropes, please. Make him feel at home. I know I can rely on you. Sit beside him, Jason, you will soon settle down. Right. Good. Carry on."

Mr Wailes left the room without either of us realising that he was spoiling our friendship. At break I was eager to meet Jason and I tried hard to make him feel welcome. He spoke with a soft, lilting Welsh accent which made us all laugh. He was immediately accepted and kept us all amused with stories of his old school. Even so, when, at the end of school, Mark asked Jason to walk home with us, I felt cheated. This was *our* time, when we laughed together, dreamed up schemes, and chewed over the day's events. Suddenly, I felt left out, and I didn't like it.

"Mark and I are going now," I stated firmly.

"Where to?" Jason enquired.

"We're going to my house," I answered.

"Can I come?"

I was about to say "No" when Mark said he would give my house a miss and show Jason the field where we played – *our* field. I left them walking off together, joking and laughing loudly. I felt stung.

It got worse over the next few days. Mark started every other sentence with, "Jason says that...", or "Me and Jason were thinking of going to...". Secretly, I boiled inside. Every sentence, every mention of his name, was like a hammer-blow. He was spoiling everything. When he talked, I felt myself scowling; when he made suggestions, I heard MY voice turning them down. One day, Mark said he was going to the cinema with Jason and that he would see me the next day.

"What about football, tonight?" I asked.

"It can wait," he replied, "I want to see this film, it's supposed to be brilliant."

The next day, they were full of stories about the night before. They talked about it all the way to school. I was the outsider, unable to join in or to get their attention. I hated it. I hated being out of touch and, suddenly, I realised that I hated Jason Jones. I knew then that I would wipe that stupid grin off his face as soon as I got the chance.

In the end, my chance came a week later. We had been to Mark's house to watch a video and, when it finished, Jason and I set off for home. By now he had sensed that I didn't like him and we walked on quietly together. Inside, I was a torrent of pent-up anger, ready to explode. I resented him. Everything he said and did got under my skin and irritated me. I was looking for trouble that night. Then suddenly he spoke:

"You know, I'm not trying to spoil your friendship."

"What?"

"I just want us all to be friends." he said.

"Oh yeah!" I replied sarcastically.

"It's true. You seem to think I'm against you and want to get rid of you. I don't."

This was the excuse I had been looking for. He wanted to talk: I wanted to argue. The more reasonable he was, the more aggressive I became. He was becoming frightened and I was enjoying it. I don't even remember how we came to blows, only that I launched into him, fists pumping like the pistons of a steam-engine. It was a very one-sided contest. Days of jealousy and frustration poured out of me until I was out of control. When I left him, he was crying.

By the time that I got home, my anger had gone. I knew I had done wrong, and that I would have to face both Mark and Jason the next day at school. I now realised that Jason had been trying to put things right between us. He had wanted us to start again and I had spoilt it all.

The next day at school was worse than I could have expected. Jason's face was marked and swollen and, of course, there was a big scene with the teachers. Jason's mum had been to see Old Wailes, and it was not long before I was in his office trying to explain myself. The headteacher called me a lout and a thug. What could I say? He was right. But the worst was still to come. At break, I saw Mark as I made my way along the corridor. He saw me too, but he pretended not to. He simply put his head down and walked briskly past me.

I don't hang around with Mark anymore. I often see Jason and him on the field, laughing, talking, enjoying each other's friendship. I have new friends now, but I still miss my old friend; my best friend. I think the worst thing is that he doesn't care any more, and I have to cope with the fact that my jealousy caused it all.

I always say that Jason Jones ruined it for me, but, deep down, I know it was my own fault – and the pain that that causes is something I will have to live with.

Discussing the story

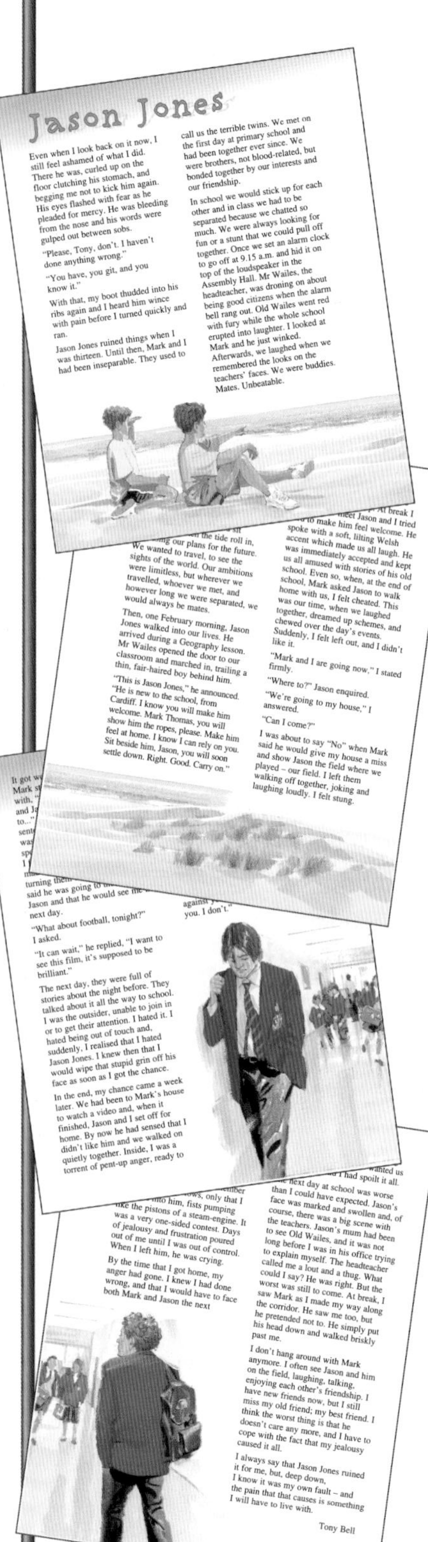

Jason Jones

Even when I look back on it now, I still feel ashamed of what I did. There he was, curled up on the floor clutching his stomach, and begging me not to kick him again. His eyes flashed with fear as he pleaded for mercy. He was bleeding from the nose and his words were gulped out between sobs.

"Please, Tony, don't. I haven't done anything wrong."

"You have, you git, and you know it."

With that, my boot thudded into his ribs again and I heard him wince with pain before I turned quickly and ran.

Jason Jones ruined things when I was thirteen. Until then, Mark and I had been inseparable. They used to call us the terrible twins. We met on the first day at primary school and had been together ever since. We were brothers, not blood-related, but bonded together by our interests and our friendship.

In school we would stick up for each other and in class we had to be separated because we chatted so much. We were always looking for fun or a stunt that we could pull off together. Once we set an alarm clock to go off at 9.15 a.m. and hid it on top of the loudspeaker in the Assembly Hall. Mr Wailes, the headteacher, was droning on about being good citizens when the alarm bell rang out. Old Wailes went red with fury while the whole school erupted into laughter. I looked at Mark and he just winked. Afterwards, we laughed when we remembered the looks on the teachers' faces. We were buddies. Mates. Unbeatable.

... the tide roll in, ... our plans for the future. We wanted to travel, to see the sights of the world. Our ambitions were limitless, but wherever we travelled, whoever we met, and however long we were separated, we would always be mates.

Then, one February morning, Jason Jones walked into our lives. He arrived during a Geography lesson. Mr Wailes opened the door to our classroom and marched in, trailing a thin, fair-haired boy behind him.

"This is Jason Jones," he announced. "He is new to the school, from Cardiff. I know you will make him welcome. Mark Thomas, you will show him the ropes, please. Make him feel at home. I know I can rely on you. Sit beside him, Jason, you will soon settle down. Right. Good. Carry on."

... At break I ... meet Jason and I tried ... to make him feel welcome. He spoke with a soft, lilting Welsh accent which made us all laugh. He was immediately accepted and kept us all amused with stories of his old school. Even so, when, at the end of school, Mark asked Jason to walk home with us, I felt cheated. This was our time, when we laughed together, dreamed up schemes, and chewed over the day's events. Suddenly, I felt left out, and I didn't like it.

"Mark and I are going now," I stated firmly.

"Where to?" Jason enquired.

"We're going to my house," I answered.

"Can I come?"

I was about to say "No" when Mark said he would give my house a miss and show Jason the field where we played – our field. I left them walking off together, joking and laughing loudly. I felt stung.

It got w... Mark st... with, "... and Ja... to..." sent... was... sp... I ... turning them ... said he was going to ... Jason and that he would see me ... next day.

"What about football, tonight?" I asked.

"It can wait," he replied, "I want to see this film, it's supposed to be brilliant."

The next day, they were full of stories about the night before. They talked about it all the way to school. I was the outsider, unable to join in or to get their attention. I hated it. I hated being out of touch and, suddenly, I realised that I hated Jason Jones. I knew then that I would wipe that stupid grin off his face as soon as I got the chance.

In the end, my chance came a week later. We had been to Mark's house to watch a video and, when it finished, Jason and I set off for home. By now he had sensed that I didn't like him and we walked on quietly together. Inside, I was a torrent of pent-up anger, ready to

... against ... you. I don't."

... ember ... ows, only that I ... into him, fists pumping like the pistons of a steam-engine. It was a very one-sided contest. Days of jealousy and frustration poured out of me until I was out of control. When I left him, he was crying.

By the time that I got home, my anger had gone. I knew I had done wrong, and that I would have to face both Mark and Jason the next

... wanted us ... I had spoilt it all.

... next day at school was worse than I could have expected. Jason's face was marked and swollen and, of course, there was a big scene with the teachers. Jason's mum had been to see Old Wailes, and it was not long before I was in his office trying to explain myself. The headteacher called me a lout and a thug. What could I say? He was right. But the worst was still to come. At break, I saw Mark as I made my way along the corridor. He saw me too, but he pretended not to. He simply put his head down and walked briskly past me.

I don't hang around with Mark anymore. I often see Jason and him on the field, laughing, talking, enjoying each other's friendship. I have new friends now, but I still miss my old friend; my best friend. I think the worst thing is that he doesn't care any more, and I have to cope with the fact that my jealousy caused it all.

I always say that Jason Jones ruined it for me, but, deep down, I know it was my own fault – and the pain that that causes is something I will have to live with.

Tony Bell

Task

Read the story *Jason Jones*.

Talk about the story with at least one other person.

How?

During your discussion, talk about what happened in the story. Use the following statements to help you. Read each one and decide whether it is true or false:

- **A** Tony was upset by what he did to Jason.
- **B** Tony walked away after he beat Jason.
- **C** Mark and Tony met on their first day at school.
- **D** Mr Wailes was in Assembly when the alarm clock rang.
- **E** Mark and Tony went on holiday to Wales.
- **F** Mr Wailes asked Tony to look after Jason in school.
- **G** At first, Tony liked Jason.
- **H** Tony did not like Jason spending so much time with his friend Mark.
- **I** On the night of the fight, Tony and Jason had been playing football.
- **J** Jason wanted to be friends with Tony.
- **K** Tony had to see the headteacher on the day after the fight.
- **L** Mark told Tony that he was wrong to fight with Jason.
- **M** Mark, Tony and Jason are all friends now.

Tips for success

- Make sure you understand the tasks.
- Making notes before the discussion may help you to remember the things you want to talk about.
- Use the How? box to help you through the activity.
- Speak clearly.
- Explain carefully.
- Listen to others.
- Take turns.

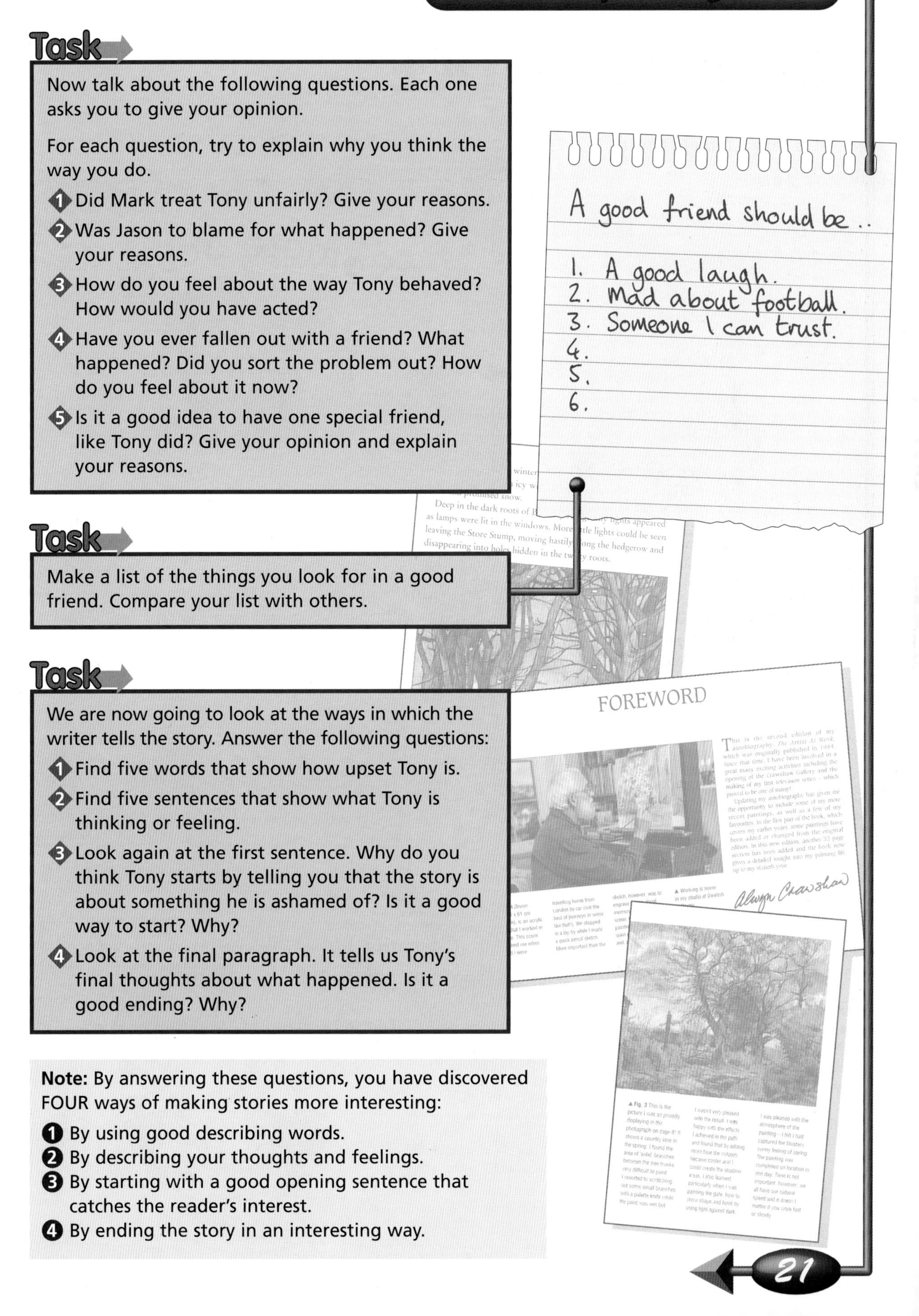

Task

Now talk about the following questions. Each one asks you to give your opinion.

For each question, try to explain why you think the way you do.

1. Did Mark treat Tony unfairly? Give your reasons.
2. Was Jason to blame for what happened? Give your reasons.
3. How do you feel about the way Tony behaved? How would you have acted?
4. Have you ever fallen out with a friend? What happened? Did you sort the problem out? How do you feel about it now?
5. Is it a good idea to have one special friend, like Tony did? Give your opinion and explain your reasons.

Task

Make a list of the things you look for in a good friend. Compare your list with others.

Task

We are now going to look at the ways in which the writer tells the story. Answer the following questions:

1. Find five words that show how upset Tony is.
2. Find five sentences that show what Tony is thinking or feeling.
3. Look again at the first sentence. Why do you think Tony starts by telling you that the story is about something he is ashamed of? Is it a good way to start? Why?
4. Look at the final paragraph. It tells us Tony's final thoughts about what happened. Is it a good ending? Why?

Note: By answering these questions, you have discovered FOUR ways of making stories more interesting:

1. By using good describing words.
2. By describing your thoughts and feelings.
3. By starting with a good opening sentence that catches the reader's interest.
4. By ending the story in an interesting way.

TOMATO SAUCE

Here is a story written for very young children.
It is called *Tomato Sauce*.

I tapped it on the bottom.
3

Nothing came out.
4

I tried to push my fork in.
5

Still nothing came out.
I smacked it as hard as I could.
7
Everything came out, every little drop.
8

Discussing the story

Task

Read the story *Tomato Sauce.*

With at least one other person, talk about what you have learnt about books for young children.

How?

Look at both the words and the pictures. Writers often use pictures to give children of this age a better understanding of the story. Think about:

- **A** The face of the character, and the emotions that are shown.
- **B** The way the pictures are drawn, especially the colours and shapes.
- **C** Where the story takes place.
- **D** The number of words on a page.
- **E** The difficulty of the words used.
- **F** What children might learn from this story.

Research

Find other examples of books written for young children.

Use the notes in the How? box to help you to think about the way that writers set out their stories.

How are these other books like *Tomato Sauce?*

How are they different from it?

Tips for success

- Make sure you understand the tasks.
- Making notes before the discussion may help you to remember the things you want to talk about.
- Use the How? box to help you through the activity.
- Speak clearly.
- Explain carefully.
- Listen to others.
- Take turns.

Planning your story

You have looked at two pieces of writing. You now know that stories may be written in different ways. Choose one of these tasks:

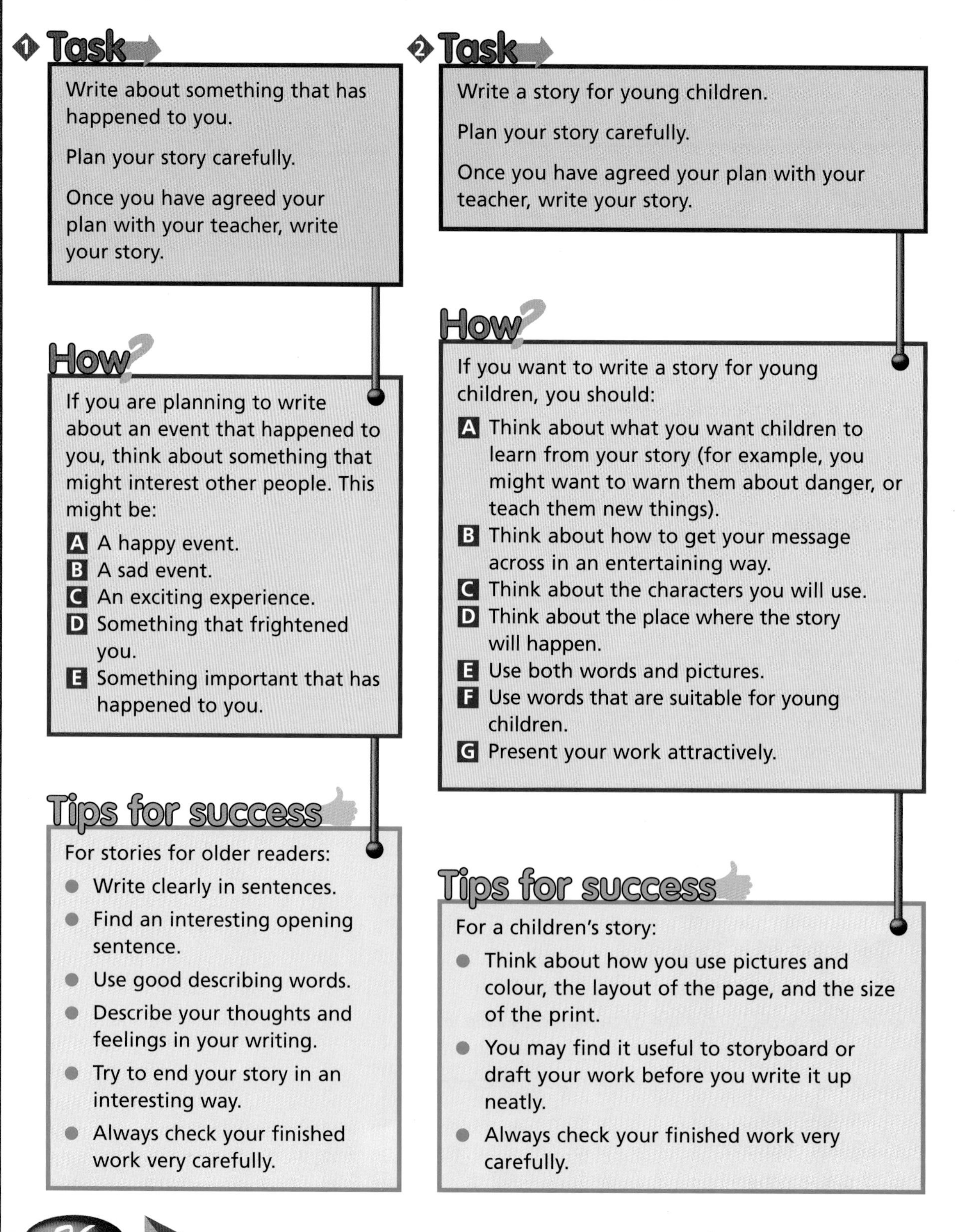

1 Task

Write about something that has happened to you.

Plan your story carefully.

Once you have agreed your plan with your teacher, write your story.

How?

If you are planning to write about an event that happened to you, think about something that might interest other people. This might be:

- **A** A happy event.
- **B** A sad event.
- **C** An exciting experience.
- **D** Something that frightened you.
- **E** Something important that has happened to you.

Tips for success

For stories for older readers:

- Write clearly in sentences.
- Find an interesting opening sentence.
- Use good describing words.
- Describe your thoughts and feelings in your writing.
- Try to end your story in an interesting way.
- Always check your finished work very carefully.

2 Task

Write a story for young children.

Plan your story carefully.

Once you have agreed your plan with your teacher, write your story.

How?

If you want to write a story for young children, you should:

- **A** Think about what you want children to learn from your story (for example, you might want to warn them about danger, or teach them new things).
- **B** Think about how to get your message across in an entertaining way.
- **C** Think about the characters you will use.
- **D** Think about the place where the story will happen.
- **E** Use both words and pictures.
- **F** Use words that are suitable for young children.
- **G** Present your work attractively.

Tips for success

For a children's story:

- Think about how you use pictures and colour, the layout of the page, and the size of the print.
- You may find it useful to storyboard or draft your work before you write it up neatly.
- Always check your finished work very carefully.

Task

Read your story to at least one other person.

Tips for success

- Reading a story aloud properly needs a lot of practice.
- Read the story over a few times before you read aloud.
- Read slowly and clearly.
- Make sure you read loudly enough.
- Try to put some feeling into your reading.
- Make sure you show any pictures from the story.

Work

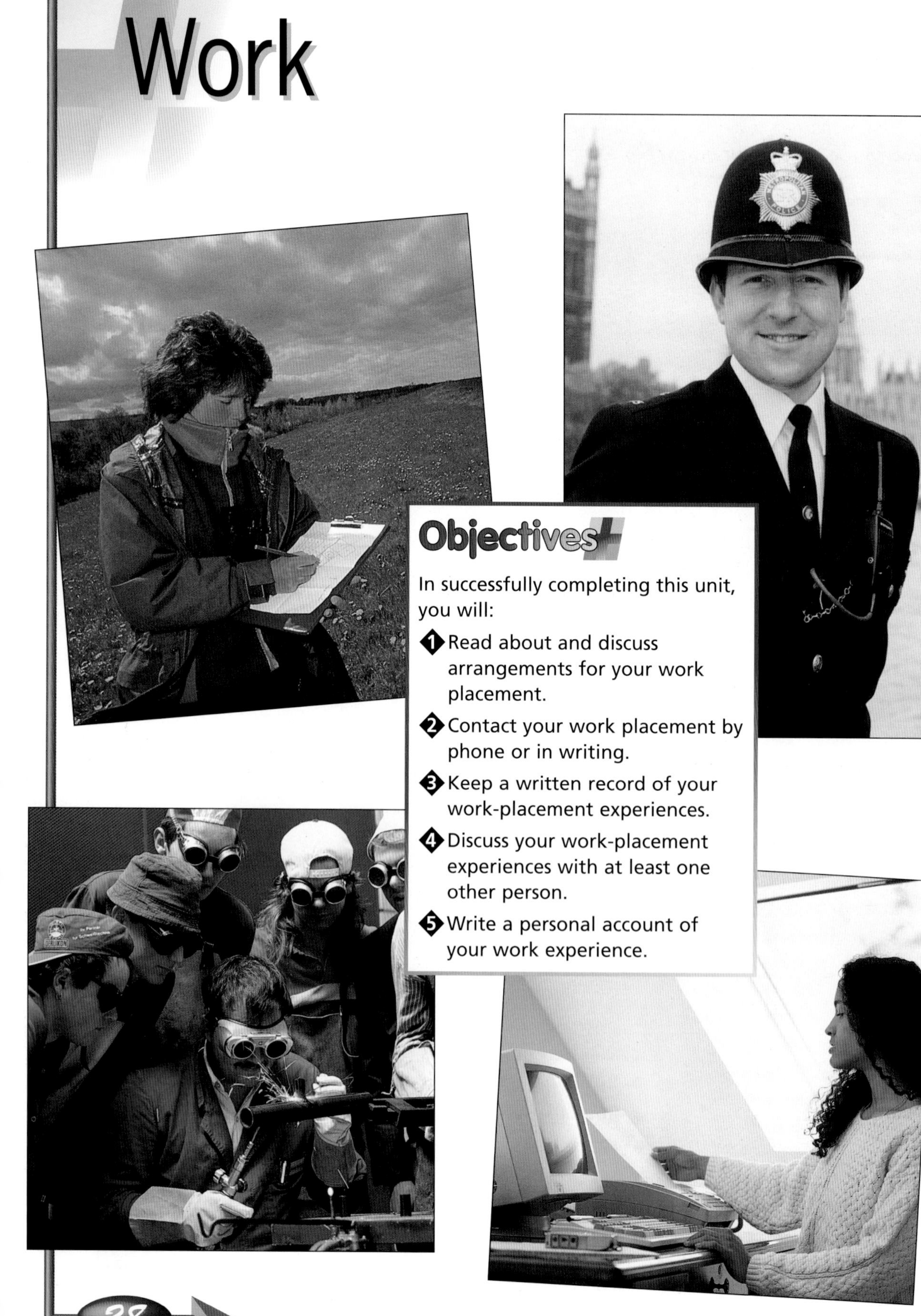

Objectives

In successfully completing this unit, you will:

1. Read about and discuss arrangements for your work placement.
2. Contact your work placement by phone or in writing.
3. Keep a written record of your work-placement experiences.
4. Discuss your work-placement experiences with at least one other person.
5. Write a personal account of your work experience.

Introduction

In this unit, you are going to prepare yourself for work placement. You will then keep a written record of your experiences during your placement and use your notes to present a final report to class.

Task

Look at the pictures on the previous page.

Discuss what information they give about the types of work they show.

How?

During your discussion, you might talk about:

A WHERE the work is taking place (inside or outside, in a factory or in an office).
B WHAT KIND of work is being done (work with tools, machines or people).
C WHAT KIND of clothing the people are wearing.
D WHY you think they are dressed in this way.
E WHICH of the jobs shown you like best – and why.

Tips for success

- Make sure you understand the tasks.
- Making notes before the discussion may help you to remember the things you want to talk about.
- Use the How? box to help you through the activity.
- Speak clearly.
- Explain carefully.
- Listen to others.
- Take turns.

Research

Talk to two people you know who have a job.

Find out about the kind of work they do.

Do they have to dress in a particular way? Why?

Are there any special precautions they have to take to take in doing their job? Why?

Planning your placement

You are planning to go out on your work experience placement. To make it as successful as possible, the following pages will help you to prepare.

To begin with, you will need to have some basic information about your placement.

This will include finding out about:

- Where your placement is.
- The type of work you will be doing.
- Any necessary travel arrangements.
- The hours you will be working (for example, 9.00 a.m. to 5.30 p.m.).
- Dress code.
- Any health and safety rules.

You may be given some of this information in school. You may have to find out some of it for yourself.

In order to gather the information together, you may find it helpful to write down the details on a sheet of paper.

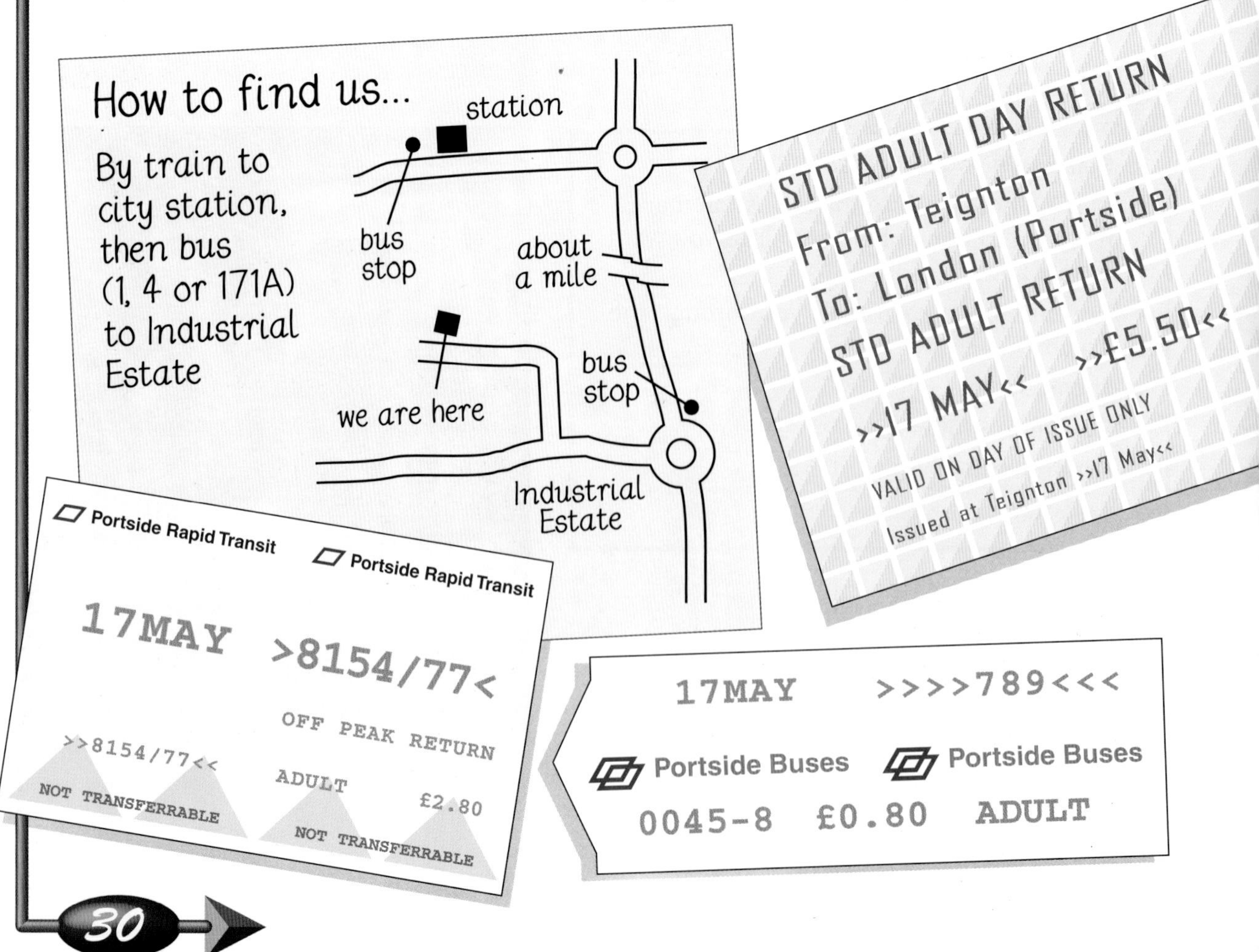

Making notes

Task

Design your own work experience information sheet.

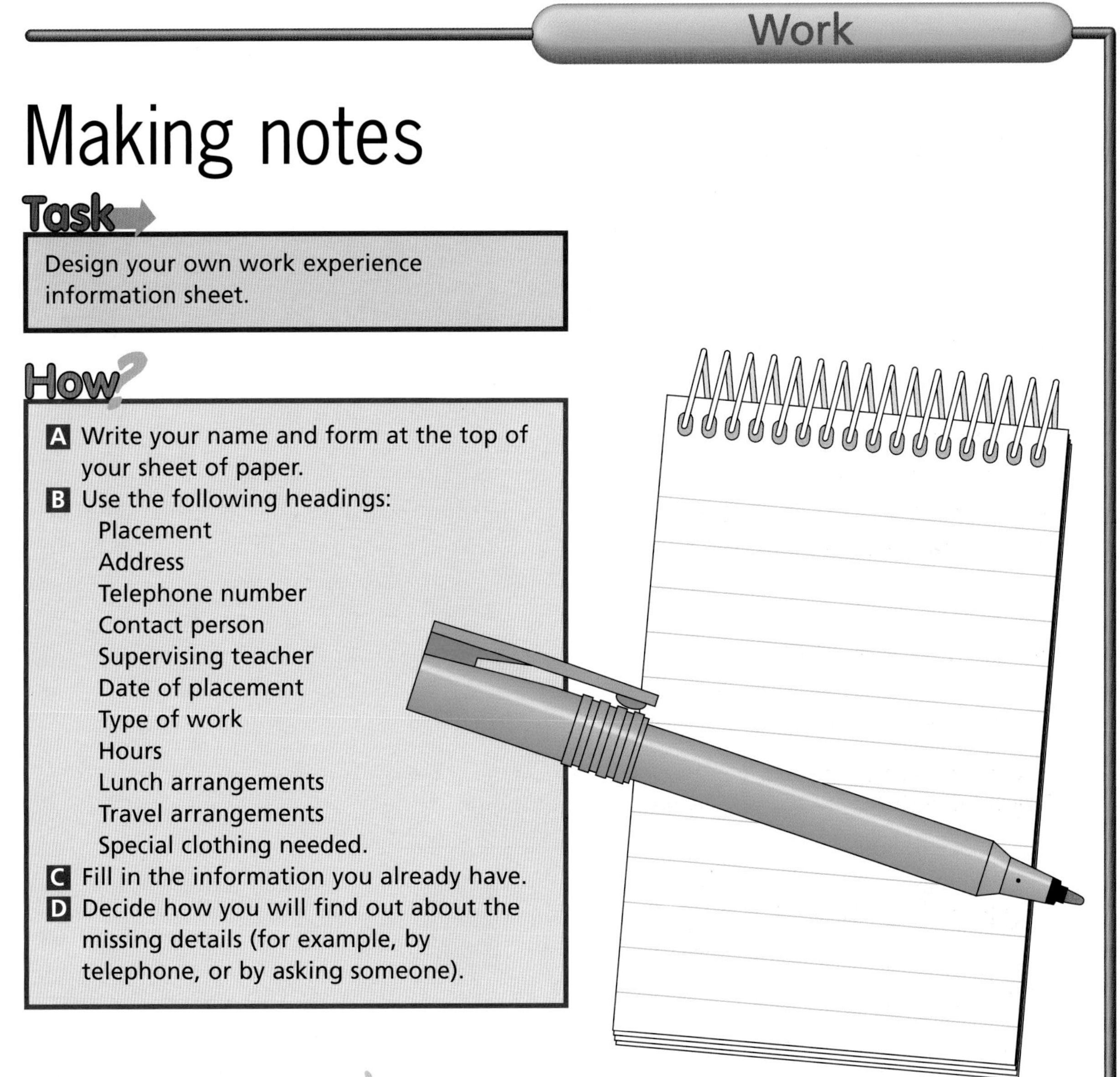

How?

A Write your name and form at the top of your sheet of paper.

B Use the following headings:
- Placement
- Address
- Telephone number
- Contact person
- Supervising teacher
- Date of placement
- Type of work
- Hours
- Lunch arrangements
- Travel arrangements
- Special clothing needed.

C Fill in the information you already have.

D Decide how you will find out about the missing details (for example, by telephone, or by asking someone).

Tips for success

Writing:

- Do not write anything until you are sure of the information you are looking for.
- Write neatly in blue or black ink.

Using the telephone:

- If you are using a pay-phone, make sure you have enough change for the call. It might be a good idea to buy a phone-card.
- Make a list of the details you need to find out.
- Have pen and paper ready to note down the answers.
- Ask to speak to the contact person whose name you have been given.
- Introduce yourself clearly.
- Say why you are calling.
- Speak clearly.
- Listen carefully.
- Note down the answers as you go along.
- If in doubt, ask for the answer to be repeated.
- When you have the information you need, thank your contact before ending the call.

Letters

For many of you, this will be your first experience of working life outside school.

You will find many differences:

- You will be working with adults.
- You will be given responsibility.
- You will be working longer hours.

Sometimes, you may find that you are unsure about how to respond in certain situations.

The following pages contain a selection of letters which describe some of these situations. They are taken from a school magazine. They may help to prepare you for events that could occur on your work experience.

Task

Read all of the letters.

Dear Editor,

I have just finished the first week of my work experience at Althorpe's Cake Shop in the centre of Leaham. I was really looking forward to having a good time away from school for a couple of weeks, but it has turned out to be the most boring thing I have ever done.

The people I am working with are both quite old (over 40!) so we don't have a lot to talk about, and they are always moaning about teenagers today.

Another thing is that the shop is only really busy over the lunch-time period, so I spend most of the day just standing around.

Can you suggest anything I could do to make the second week more interesting?

Yours, in desperation,

Jenny Lithgoe

Dear Editor,

I have recently finished my work placement at Johnson's the electrical shop in the High Street. It was great. The sales assistants were friendly and helpful and the Manager was very encouraging. On the last day they gave me a card and a box of chocolates. I want to say thank you. Any ideas?

Yours faithfully

Sheela Varghese 11C

Dear Editor,

I have been working at Mick's Garage in Leaham Old Road as a garage mechanic. I like the work and I have tried very hard to impress but I am having real trouble with two of the apprentices.

Because I am new, they constantly tease and make fun of me. On the first day I was sent to the stores for a skyhook and saw the funny side of it. However, the last two days have been worrying. They keep talking about having to pass "the apprentice's test". This means having to be held down while I am covered in engine grease. They also push me or thump me and then laugh. I can take a joke but this just isn't funny. What should I do? I don't want to be a spoilsport but I don't want to be made a fool either.

Yours faithfully

Gareth Thomas 11A

Dear Editor,

I have recently done work experience as a Clerical Assistant in the offices of Dexley's Paper Mill in Leaham Business Park.

I enjoyed the work very much as I was able to learn about using computers to keep records and other sorts of information. What I wasn't happy about was the way some of the men who worked there treated me.

One in particular became a real nuisance. At first I thought he was just being friendly and helping me because I was new. Then he started telling me rude jokes and asking me to sit on his knee.

By the end of the first week he was constantly finding excuses to be wherever I was – usually when other people weren't around. Sometimes he would follow me into one of the file-stores and he would end up touching me 'by accident'. It really made me feel very scared, so I was pleased when the placement ended. I didn't mention it to the bosses because I wasn't sure they would believe me and if I tell my dad, he will just go down and thump the man. Do you have any suggestions about what I could have done?

Yours faithfully,

Paula Timms

Dear Editor
Next week I am going on my work placement to MidWest Bank in Leaham Old Road. I am not looking forward to it. I do not mix easily with other people and my mum says I am shy. The truth is I lack self-confidence and I am worried I might not be able to do the work or to get on with adults. I am not sure what to say to older people and I am terrified of being left alone on the desk to deal with members of the public in case I make a mistake. My teacher says I am worrying too much and my mum says I will soon fit in. I am not so sure. What advice do you have for me? I am particularly worried about the first day. Is there anything I can do or say to make life easier?

Yours Faithfully
Darren Andrews

Dear Editor
Last week I finished my placement as a joiner. I really liked it. I was given lots of responsibility and enjoyed working with other joiners. We made window frames and fitted kitchens on a new estate. Now, I am really interested in a career in this kind of work. How do I get started? Will I need qualifications? Will I have to study at college? Please give me some advice.

Yours faithfully
Brendan O'Hara

Writing your reply

Task

Choose one of the letters on pages 33–35 to discuss with someone else.

Write a response to one of the letters, offering advice about how to deal with the problem described in the letter.

Dear Sheela,

Stay calm.

How?

- A Read each letter at least twice.
- B Choose to work on the letter that interests you most.
- C Identify and discuss the problem with at least one other person.
- D Think and talk about possible solutions.
- E Choose what you think is the best advice to give.

Dear Darren,

It's OK.

Dear Sinead,

Don't worry!

Dear Jamila,

Tell a teacher

Dear Chris,

Ask your careers advisor.

Dear Ramon,

Try again...

Tips for success

When discussing the letters:

- Talk clearly.
- Listen carefully.
- Take turns.
- Making notes may help you to remember the things to write in your letter later.

When writing your reply:

- Be clear in the advice you give.
- Explain the reasons for the advice you give.
- Write in sentences.
- Write neatly
- Write a draft of the letter so that you can get it right before you do your final version.

Health and safety

You should be aware that all workplaces have rules about health and safety.

Sometimes, symbols are used to warn of possible danger. It is important that you understand what these symbols mean.

Here are some examples.

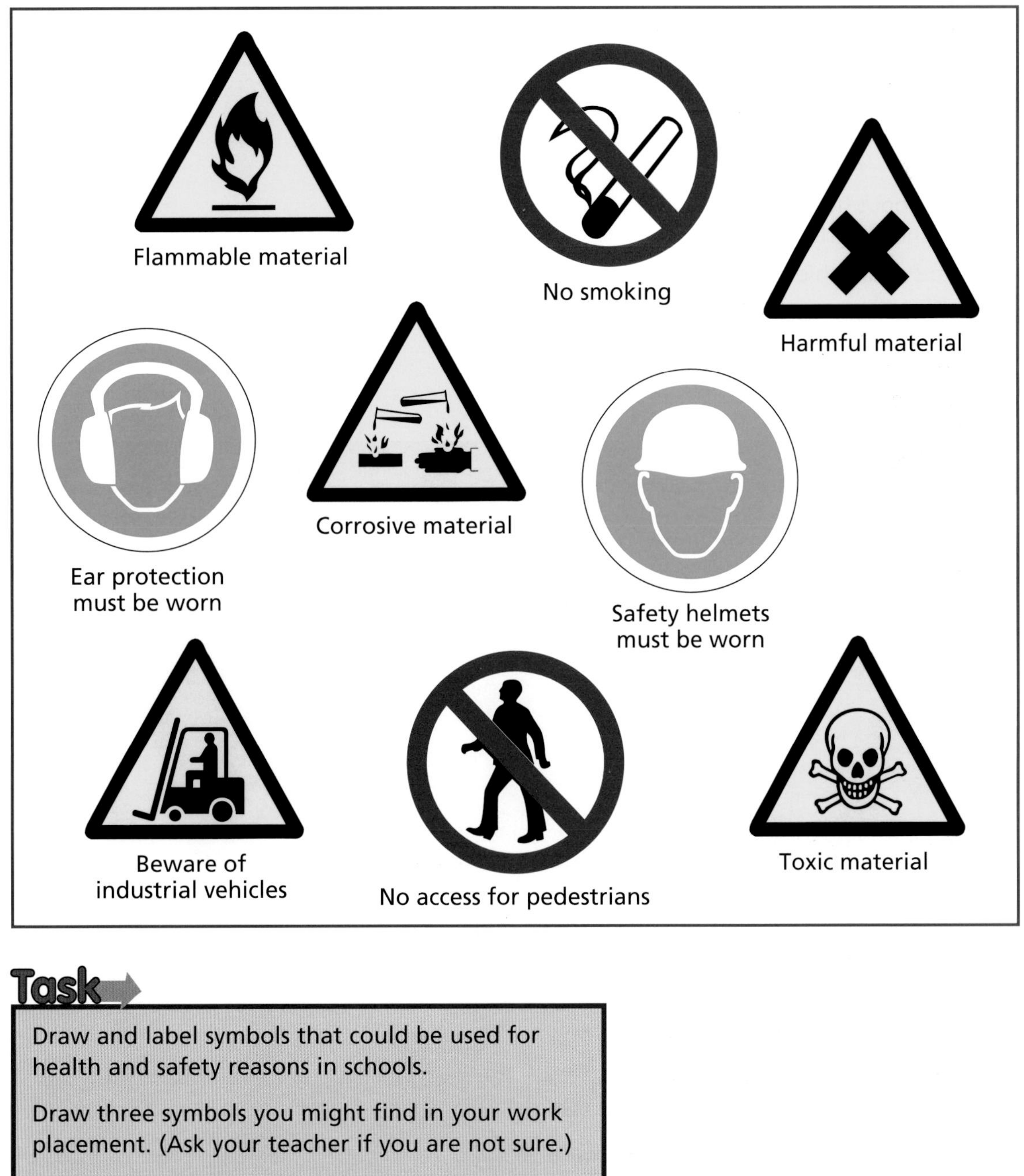

Task

Draw and label symbols that could be used for health and safety reasons in schools.

Draw three symbols you might find in your work placement. (Ask your teacher if you are not sure.)

Invent, draw and label five symbols you could use in your home.

Making the most of work experience

Often students forget some of the details of what happens on their work placement. You will want to make the most of your work experiences. In order to do this, you will need to:

- Collect information you will need later.
- Keep an accurate record of your experiences.
- Record your thoughts, feelings and attitudes towards a) the work you will do, and b) the people you will meet.
- Think about how you coped and what you gained from the experiences.
- Record your achievements.

On the next three pages you will find good examples of how to record this sort of information. If your teacher gives you worksheets to complete, these will help.

Recording the first day

You are likely to learn more new things during your first day than at any other time.

For example:

- You will be meeting your new work-mates.
- Finding your way around.
- Learning how to use equipment properly.

By making notes about some of these things now, you will find it easier to remember them when you write about your work experiences later. Here is an example of how to make notes about your first day.

WORK RECORD
First day – Basic details

The job being done at my placement:	The company makes aerosols.
The customers:	Big supermarkets, and some small local companies.
The names of my work-mates:	Sharon Golroy will be looking after me, but I also met Ashraf Sadek, Ali El Mahdv and Brian Roberts.
What they do:	Sharon and Ashraf work in the office, dealing with administration. Ali is the Personnel Officer, and Brian is the Supervisor in the factory.
In an accident I should report to:	Sharon is trained in First Aid.
First impressions:	The factory is noisy and very busy, but the offices are friendly and bright. My workmates seem OK, but I can't tell yet.
The work I did:	Today I was just shown around. I hope to get to do a bit of everything eventually.
How I coped:	**With the work:** Not much to do today. **Meeting new people:** Hard to remember who everyone is. **Working with adults:** I couldn't always join in the conversations, but Ali likes football, so I talked to him at lunch.
What I liked most:	Getting out of school!
What I liked least:	Having to get up at 7.30 to get to the placement on time.

Overall: Enjoyable ☐ Better than I thought ☑ Awful ☐

Updating your records

Your teacher will offer advice about how often you need to update your records. Try to include both the things you do, and your thoughts and feelings about them. Here is an example to help you.

WORK RECORD
Up-date

Day: Monday

Date: June 23rd

Today I worked in: (e.g. office/workshop) Reception

My tasks were:
Answering the phone.
Dealing with the public.
Making tea and coffee.

I watched others doing:
Sending faxes.
Filing.
Typing.

I enjoyed:
Answering the phone.

I did not enjoy / found difficult
Making the tea – horrible!

My feelings about my placement now are:
Pretty boring day, but still enjoying the placement.

Final thoughts

By the end of your work experience, you will have formed clearer opinions about work and how you coped. You will need to make a note of any final thoughts. Here is an example of how you might write about your experiences.

WORK RECORD – Final thoughts

On the placement:

Things I learned:	Learned to use the photocopier, fax, and how to send e-mails.
Things I enjoyed:	Using the computer.
Things I liked most:	Meeting new people.
Things I liked least:	Filing and stock control.

About work:

Five things I have learned about working life are:

1. You have to be on time.
2. You have to ask if you are not sure about anything.
3. You need to get on with others.
4. You have to do your share of the work.
5. You have to follow the rules.

My attitudes and abilities:

I have learned that I am good at:	Using the computer.
I have learned that I need to improve on:	My time-keeping.

The future:

Following my work experience, my plans for the future are:	To work in an office.
I want to do this because:	I liked working with other people. I liked the computer work and learning how to use all the office equipment. In the office I worked in everybody helped one another and there were always lots of different things to do.

Tips for success

Before you leave, try to collect as much additional information (for example, leaflets, brochures, health and safety information) as you can.

Back to school

Now that you have completed what we hope was a successful work placement, you are going to do three things to complete this unit:

- Share your experiences with at least one other person.
- Write a letter of thanks to your work experience contact – it is good manners to do this.
- Use the information you have collected and your notes to write about your work experience.

Task

Talk with at least one other person about the time you spent on your work experience.

How?

During your discussion, you might talk about:

A The place where you worked.
B The tasks you were given.
C The people you worked with.
D Your experiences with any customers you met (include anything funny or unusual that happened).
E What you learned.
F Your thoughts about the work.
G Your thoughts about your future.

Tips for success

- Make sure you understand the task.
- Making notes before the discussion may help you to remember the things you want to talk about.
- Use the How? box to help you through the activity.
- Speak clearly.
- Explain carefully.
- Listen to others.
- Take turns.

A letter of thanks

Task

Write a letter of thanks and address an envelope to your work placement contact.

How?

Here is an example of how you might set out your letter.

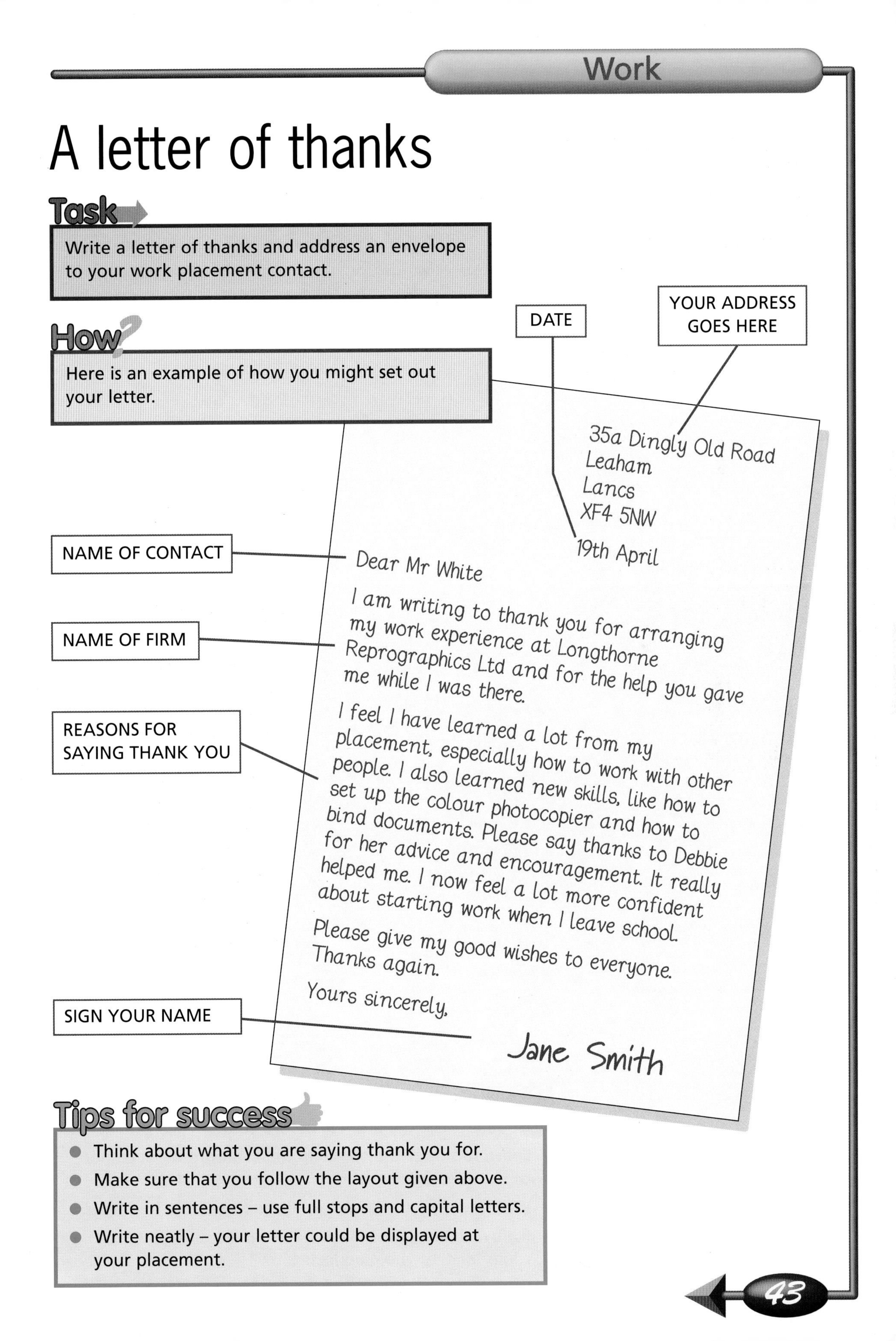

Tips for success

- Think about what you are saying thank you for.
- Make sure that you follow the layout given above.
- Write in sentences – use full stops and capital letters.
- Write neatly – your letter could be displayed at your placement.

Addressing the envelope

Here is an example of how to set out your envelope.

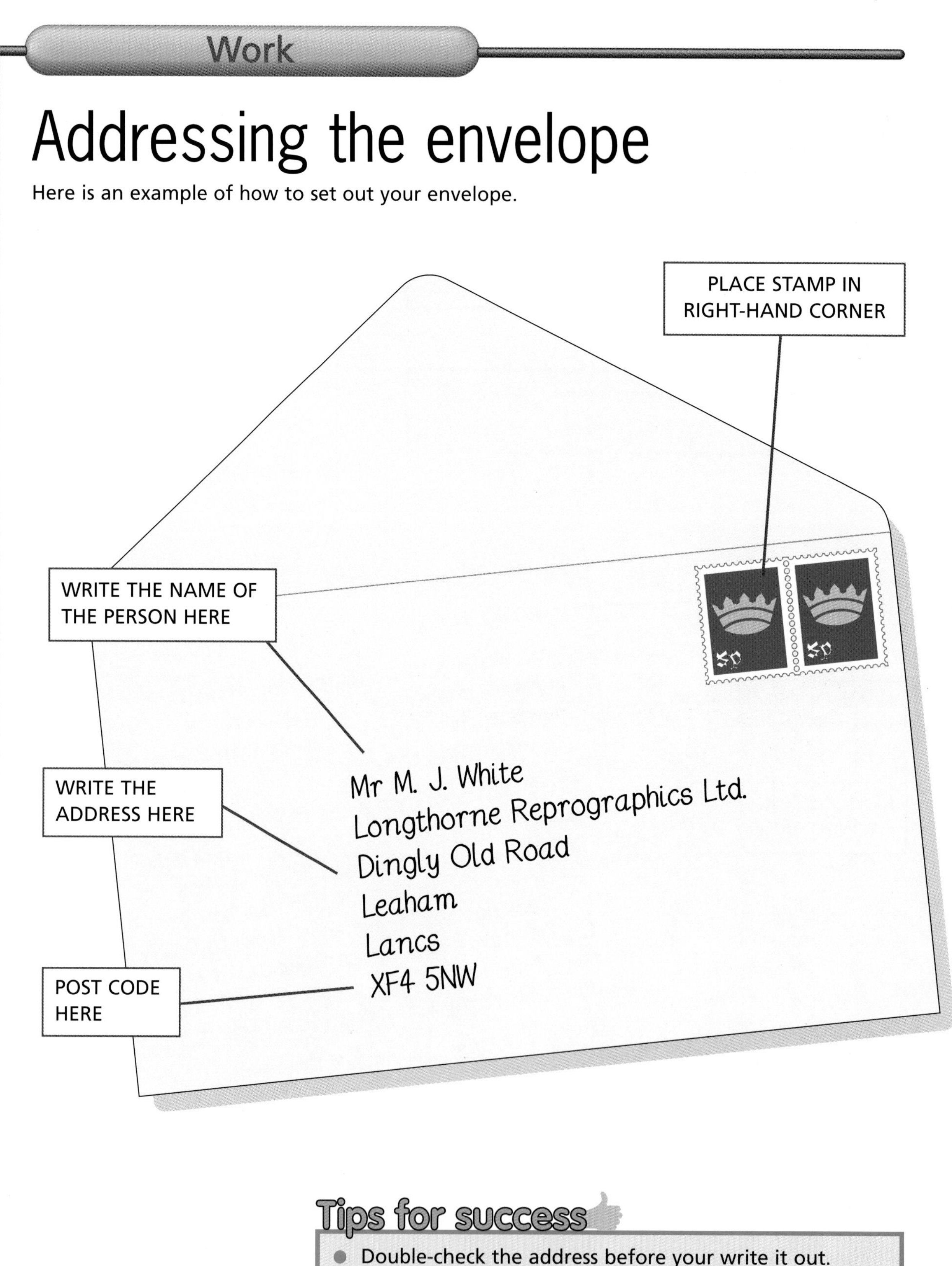

Tips for success

- Double-check the address before your write it out.
- Leave room for the stamp in the top right-hand corner of the envelope.
- Write neatly – the postman needs to be able to read it.
- Follow the layout shown above – make sure you have room for the whole address.

Writing your report

Task

Write about what you thought of your work placement.

How?

When planning your report:

- **A** Look again at your notes and any other material from your placement.
- **B** Make a note of the important things you did.
- **C** Note down any things that you feel you have learnt about the world of work.
- **D** Note any change in the way you think about yourself and what you want to do in the future.

When writing your report:

- **A** Begin with a brief account of where you went and what you did.
- **B** Use your plan to help you to organise your thoughts in writing.
- **C** In the last paragraph, write about your overall view of your work experience and about your hopes for your future.

Tips for success

- Planning comes first.
- Be clear about what you are going to write.
- Write in sentences.
- Use full stops and capital letters.
- Start a new paragraph for each part of your plan.
- Write neatly.
- Write a draft version of your report and read through it to correct any mistakes, before writing your final version.

Reading for pleasure

ELIZABETH HAND
GLIMMERING
A NOVEL OF THE COMING MILLENNIUM

ANITA AND ME • MEERA SYAL

'Tom Sawyer meets Cider With Rosie en route to India via Wolverhampton. A wonderful book – treat yourself.'
Ben Elton

Objectives

In successfully completing this unit, you will:

1. Read and talk about a story.
2. Discuss the types of people you have read about in the story.
3. Read and talk about three poems.
4. Talk about how one of the pieces of writing makes you feel.
5. Produce a piece of writing based on the story or one of the poems that you have read.

A BIOGRAPHY

HUMPHREY CARPENTER
'ONE OF THE MOST INTERESTING AND READABLE BIOGRAPHIES OF A LITERARY FIGURE FOR SOME TIME'

THE NEW SCIENCE OF FUZZY LOGIC
Fuzzy Thinking
Bart Kosko
'An exciting and truly revolutionary book'
Danah Zohar, INDEPENDENT ON SUNDAY

ARTHUR C. CLARKE
2061
ODYSSEY THREE
'HUGELY READABLE' NEW SCIENTIST

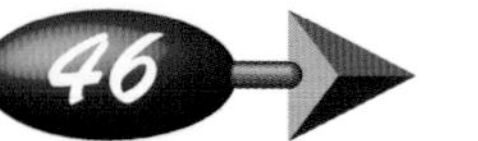

Introduction

In this unit you are going to read and discuss one story and three poems. You will then produce a piece of writing based on the story or on one of the poems.

Task

Look at the pictures on the previous page.

Discuss the different types of book covers shown.

How?

During your discussion, you might talk about:

A The book titles that interest you most.
B Which cover you think is best – and why.
C The different types of reading material shown.
D What sort of people do you think might be interested in each type of writing – and why.
E The kinds of reading material you would show if you were making up the page – and why.

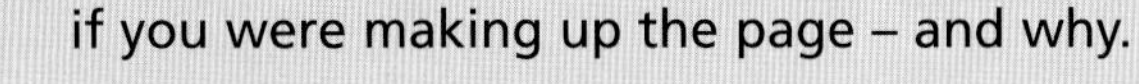

Tips for success

- Make sure you understand the tasks.
- Making notes before the discussion may help you to remember the things you want to talk about.
- Use the How? box to help you through the activity.
- Speak clearly.
- Explain carefully.
- Listen to others.
- Take turns.

The Wasteland

The moment that the bus moved on he knew he was in danger, for by the lights of it he saw the figures of the young men waiting under the tree. That was the thing feared by all, to be waited for by the young men. It was a thing he had talked about, now he was to see it for himself.

It was too late to run after the bus; it went down the dark street like an island of safety in a sea of perils. Though he had known of his danger only for a second, his mouth was already dry, his heart was pounding in his breast, something within him was crying out in protest against the coming event.

His wages were in his purse, he could feel them weigh heavily against his thigh. That was what they wanted from him. Nothing counted against that. His wife could be made a widow, his children made fatherless, nothing counted against that. Mercy was the unknown word.

While he stood there irresolute he heard the young men walking towards him, not only from the side where he had seen them, but from the other also. They did not speak; their intention was unspeakable. The sound of their feet came on the wind to him. The place was well chosen, for behind him was the high wall of the convent, and the barred door that would not open before a man was dead. On the other side of the road was the waste land, full of wire and iron, and bodies of old cars. It was his only hope, and he moved towards it; as he did so he knew from the whistle that the young men were there too …

So trapped was he that he was filled suddenly with strength and anger, and he ran towards the waste land swinging his heavy stick. In the darkness a form loomed up at him, and he swung at it, and heard it give a cry of pain. Then he plunged blindly into the wilderness of wire and iron and the bodies of old cars.

Something caught him by the leg, and he brought his stick crashing down on it, but it was no man, only some knife-edged piece of iron. He was sobbing and out of breath but he pushed on into the waste, while behind him they pushed on also, knocking against the old iron bodies and kicking against tins and buckets. He fell into some grotesque shape of wire; it was barbed and tore at his clothes and flesh. Then it held him, so that it seemed to him that death must be near, and having no other hope, he cried out, "Help, help me!" in what should have been a great voice, but was voiceless and gasping. He tore at the wire, and it tore at him too, ripping his face and his hands.

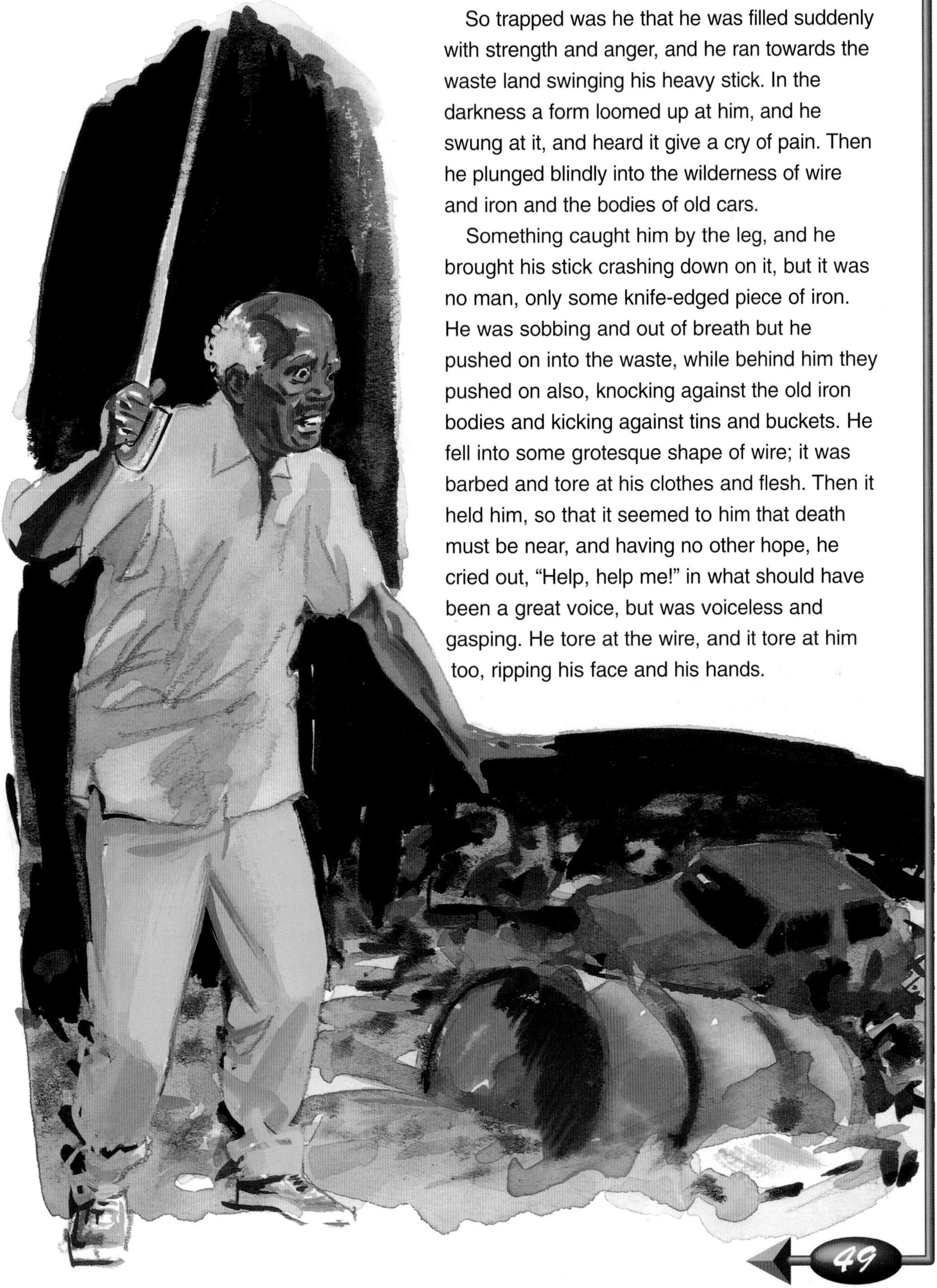

Then suddenly he was free. He saw the bus returning, and he cried out again in the great voiceless voice, "Help me, help me!" Against the lights of it he could plainly see the form of one of the young men. Death was near him, and for a moment he was filled with the injustice of life, that could end thus for one who had always been hard-working and law-abiding. He lifted the heavy stick and brought it down on the head of his pursuer so that the man crumpled to ground, moaning and groaning as though life had been unjust to him also.

Then he turned and began to run again, but ran first into the side of an old lorry which sent him reeling. He lay there for a moment expecting the blow that would end him. Even then his wits came back to him, and he turned over twice and was under the lorry. … His heart was like a wild thing in his breast, and seemed to lift his whole body each time that it beat. He tried to calm it down, thinking it might be heard, and tried to control the noise of his gasping breath, but he could not do either of these things.

Then, suddenly, against the dark sky he saw two of the young men. He thought they must hear him; but they themselves were gasping like drowned men, and their speech came by fits and starts.

Then one of them said, "Do you hear?" They were silent except for their gasping, listening. And he listened also, but could hear nothing but his own exhausted heart.

"I heard a man ... running ... on the road," said one.

"He's got away ... let's go."

Then some more of the young men came up, gasping and cursing the man who had got away.

"Freddy," said one, "your father's got away." But there was no reply.

"Where's Freddy?" one asked.

One said, "Quiet!" Then he called in a loud voice, "Freddy!" but there was still no reply.

"Let's go," he said.

They moved off slowly and carefully, then one of them stopped.

"We are saved," he said. "Here is the man."

He knelt down on the ground, and then fell to cursing.

"There's no money here," he said.

One of them lit a match, and in the small light of it the man under the lorry saw him fall back.

"It's Freddy," one said.

"He's dead."

Then the one who had said "Quiet" spoke again.

"Lift him up," he said. "Put him under the lorry."

The man under the lorry heard them struggling with the body of the dead young man, and he turned once, twice, deeper into his hiding place. The young men lifted the body and swung it under the lorry so that it touched him. Then he heard them moving away, not speaking, slowly and quietly, making an occasional sound against some obstruction in the waste.

He turned on his side, so that he would not need to touch the body of the young man. He buried his face in his arms, and said to himself in the idiom of his own language, "People, arise! The world is dead." Then he arose himself, and went heavily out of the waste land.

Alan Paton

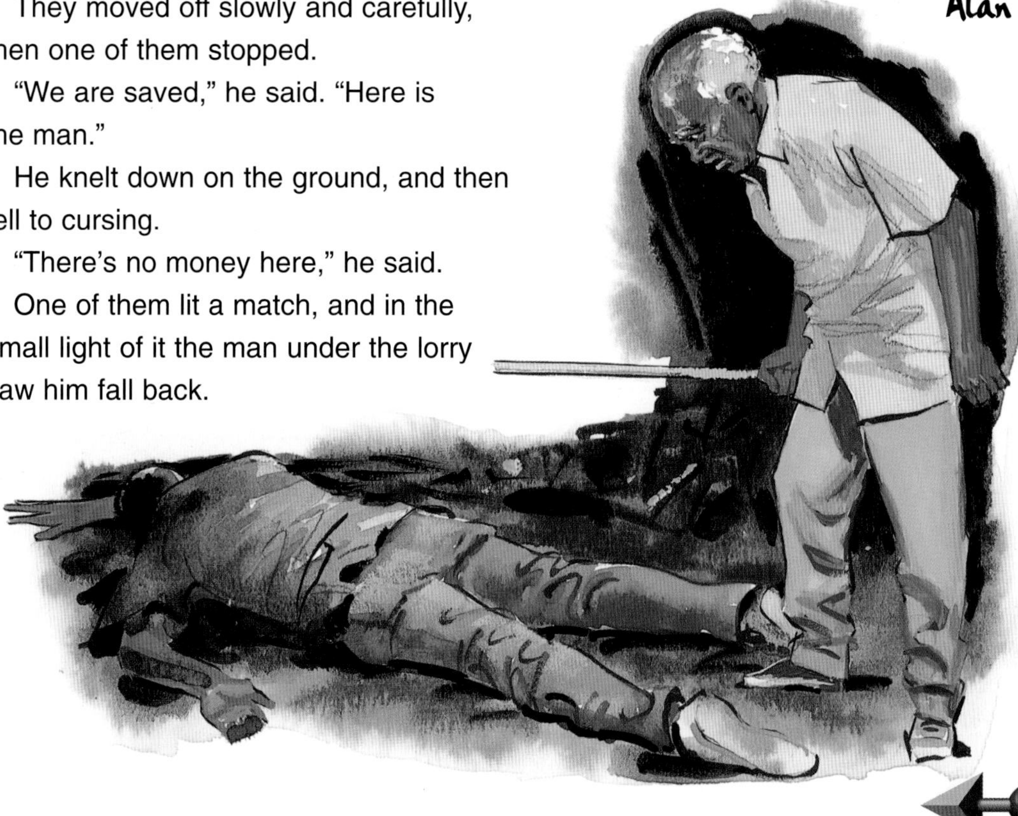

Discussing the story

Task

Read the story *The Wasteland*.

Discuss the story with at least one other person.

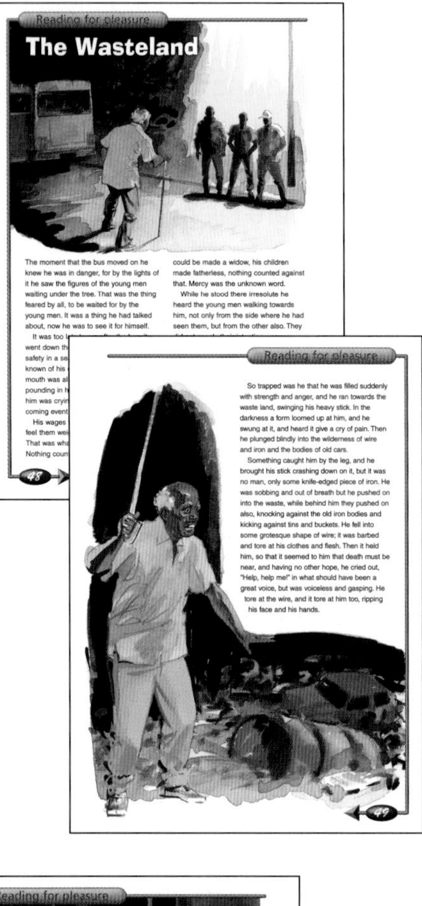

The Wasteland

The moment that the bus moved on he knew he was in danger, for by the lights of it he saw the figures of the young men waiting under the tree. That was the thing feared by all, to be waited for by the young men. It was a thing he had talked about, now he was to see it for himself.

could be made a widow, his children made fatherless, nothing counted against that. Mercy was the unknown word.

While he stood there irresolute he heard the young men walking towards him, not only from the side where he had seen them, but from the other also. They

So trapped was he that he was filled suddenly with strength and anger, and he ran towards the waste land, swinging his heavy stick. In the darkness a form loomed up at him, and he swung at it, and heard it give a cry of pain. Then he plunged blindly into the wilderness of wire and iron and the bodies of old cars.

Something caught him by the leg, and he brought his stick crashing down on it, but it was no man, only some knife-edged piece of iron. He was sobbing and out of breath but he pushed on into the waste, while behind him they pushed on also, knocking against the old iron bodies and kicking against tins and buckets. He fell into some grotesque shape of wire; it was barbed and tore at his clothes and flesh. Then it held him, so that it seemed to him that death must be near, and having no other hope, he cried out, "Help, help me!" in what should have been a great voice, but was voiceless and gasping. He tore at the wire, and it tore at him too, ripping his face and his hands.

How?

During your discussion, talk about what happened in the story. Use these questions to help you to talk about the story:

- **A** Why was the man frightened at the beginning of the story?
- **B** What did the young men want from him?
- **C** How did the man defend himself?
- **D** Why did he hit one of the young men?
- **E** Where did he hide from the gang?
- **F** Who was Freddy?
- **G** Why do you think that the gang hid Freddy's body under the lorry?
- **H** How do you think the man felt at the end of the story? Why?

Think about the language used in the story. How does the author show, for example, fear, anger or panic?

Then suddenly he was free. He saw the bus returning, and he cried out again in the great voiceless voice, "Help me, help me!" Against the lights of it he could plainly see the form of one of the young men. Death was near him, and for a moment he was filled with the injustice of life, that could end thus for one who had always been hard-working and law-abiding. He lifted the heavy stick and brought it down on the head of his pursuer so that the man crumpled to ground, moaning and groaning as though life had been unjust to him also.

Then he turned and began to run again, but ran first into the side of an old lorry which sent him reeling. He lay there for a moment expecting the blow that would end him. Even then his wits came back to him, and he turned over twice and was under the lorry. ...His heart was like a wild thing in his breast, and seemed to lift his whole body each time that it beat. He tried to calm it down, thinking it might be heard, and tried to control the noise of his gasping breath, but he could not do either of these things.

away." But there was no reply.

"Where's Freddy?" one asked.

One said, "Quiet!" Then he called in a loud voice, "Freddy!" but there was still no reply.

"Let's go," he said.

They moved off slowly and carefully, then one of them stopped.

"We are saved," he said. "Here is the man."

He knelt down on the ground, and then fell to cursing.

"There's no money here," he said.

One of them lit a match, and in the small light of it the man under the lorry saw him fall back.

He turned on his side, so that he would not need to touch the body of the young man. He buried his face in his arms, and said to himself in the idiom of his own language, "People, arise! The world is dead." Then he arose himself, and went heavily out of the waste land.

Alan Paton

Tips for success

- Make sure you understand the tasks.
- Making notes before the discussion may help you to remember the things you want to talk about.
- Use the How? box to help you through the activity.
- Speak clearly.
- Explain carefully.
- Listen to others.
- Take turns.

In Between

How's your father,
rolling in it I suppose?
Yes Mum.
Smoking his cigarettes,
drinking his wine?
Yes Mum.
Has he changed, does
he mention me?
Yes Mum.
He looks after you
well doesn't he?
Of course Mum.
I do love him, you
know that don't you?
Yes Mum.
Do you think I'm
attractive darling?
Yes Mum.
Does your father
have any friends,
girlfriends?
A few.

Is she managing to
look after you well?
Yes Dad.
In a way I still love
your mother.
Yes Dad.
Your mother isn't
taking it too
hard is she?
Not really.
She is taking care of
herself isn't she?
Yes Dad.
Does she mention
me at all?
Yes Dad.
She's a very
attractive lady.
Yes Dad.
Oh, by the way,
are you all right?
Yes Dad.

Discussing the poem

Task

Read the poem *In Between*.

Talk about the poem with at least one other person.

How?

Use these questions to help you talk about the poem:

- **A** How many people are mentioned in the poem?
- **B** What sort of things do Mum and Dad want to know?
- **C** How does the child answer Mum and Dad's questions?
- **D** Why do you think the child answers in this way?
- **E** What does Mum think about Dad and about herself?
- **F** What does Dad think about Mum and about himself?
- **G** Why do you think the poem is called *In Between*?
- **H** What do you notice about the way the two verses are set out?
- **I** What does the poem tell you about the parents' relationship with each other and with the child?

Tips for success

- Make sure you understand the tasks.
- Making notes before the discussion may help you to remember the things you want to talk about.
- Use the How? box to help you through the activity.
- Speak clearly.
- Explain carefully.
- Listen to others.
- Take turns.

Yes Mum

Yes Dad

Yes Mum

Yes Dad

My Brother

Nobody to talk to.
The bed next to me is naked –
Nobody is in it
Now he's dead.
Only five he was
Just a baby.
Whilst I write in my note book,
The wind howls
Now he's dead.

When he was a child I thought nothing of him,
But now he's dead I weep for him.
The pillow soaking wet with my tears –
I turned over.
Sad that I am, I will forget him.
Why couldn't I die instead of him?
I turned on the radio to harden my heart,
But his favourite tune is on.
I will never forget him –
He's dead now.

Philip Campbell

Discussing the poem

Task

Read the poem *My Brother.*

Talk about the poem with at least one other person.

How?

A Use the following questions to help you to talk about the poem:
- Where is the writer at the beginning of the poem?
- Why is the writer upset?
- How old was the writer's brother?
- How did the writer feel about his brother when he was alive?
- How long ago do you think the writer's brother died? Why? What clues are given in the poem?
- What sort of relationship do you think the brothers had? Why?

B Think about the language used in the poem. Which of the words and phrases help you to understand what the writer must be feeling?

C The poem describes what happens to someone when a close relative dies. Think about how well the poem deals with this subject. Is it a good description? Why?

nothing

howls

weep

nobody forget

- Make sure you understand the tasks.
- Making notes before the discussion may help you to remember the things you want to talk about.
- Use the How? box to help you through the activity.
- Speak clearly.
- Explain carefully.
- Listen to others.
- Take turns.

But You Didn't

Remember the time you lent me
your car and I dented it?
I thought you'd kill me...
But you didn't.

Remember the time I forgot to tell
you the dance was formal, and you
came in jeans?
I thought you'd hate me...
But you didn't.

Remember the times I'd
flirt with other boys just
to make you jealous,
and you were?
I thought you'd drop me...
But you didn't.

There were plenty of things
you did to put up with me,
to keep me happy, to love me,
and there are so many things
I wanted to tell you when you
returned from Vietnam...
But you didn't.

Merrill Glass

Discussing the poem

Task

Read the poem *But You Didn't.*

Talk about the poem with at least one other person.

How?

Use the following questions to help you to talk about the poem:

A Who is the writer talking about?
B What sorts of things does she remember about him?
C What kind of person was he?
D Why was she not able to tell him how she felt?
E What sort of mood is she in at the end of the poem?
F Think about the way the poem is written. What do you notice about the way each verse begins and ends?

Tips for success

- Make sure you understand the tasks.
- Making notes before the discussion may help you to remember the things you want to talk about.
- Use the How? box to help you through the activity.
- Speak clearly.
- Explain carefully.
- Listen to others.
- Take turns.

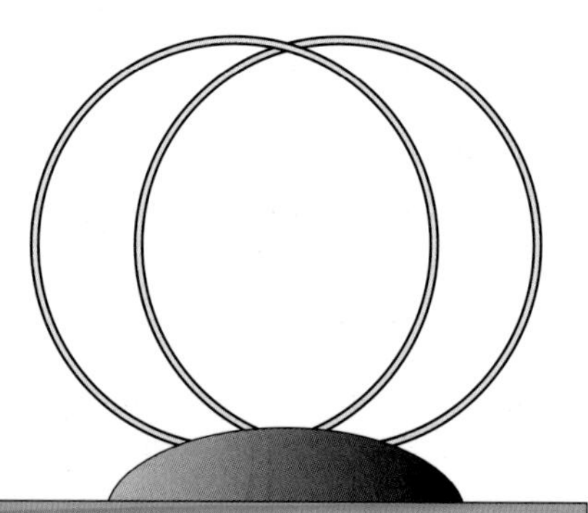

Research

The poem mentions the Vietnam war. What information can you find about this war? You could:

Look up some more information in the library.

Look up some more information on a CD-ROM.

Talk to your History teacher and others.

Find another poem which deals with loss, death or sadness.

...And finally

Now that you have read the short story and the three poems, you are going to do some writing of your own.

Task

Choose at least one of the following:

Write the story about the man's journey home from *The Wasteland* and how he explains what has happened to his wife.

Write the statement that the man might make to the police about what happens in the story *The Wasteland*.

Write the letter that the boy in the poem *My Brother* might send to an agony aunt page in a magazine, describing what has happened, explaining his feelings, and seeking advice. Then write the reply he might receive.

Write a playscipt in which the child in the poem *In Between* meets and talks with a friend about the situation with his or her parents

---

Imagine that you are the girl in the poem *But You Didn't*. Describe one of the occasions mentioned in the first three verses. Try to write a detailed story that includes how the girl felt about what happened at the time.

Tips for success

- Choose to work on the story or poem that you enjoyed reading the most.
- Re-read the story or poem before you begin.
- Use any notes that you made during the discussions to help you.
- Write a draft version of your work and correct any mistakes that you find before you present your finished work.
- Check details, such as names or events, carefully.

Media

SATURDAY Times
The Life and Soul of Glasgow
GRAB YOUR SHARE OF £50,000
THE GALS WHO'VE ALL BEEN PALS OF AL
Glasgow girls in serious cat fight
LEGENDS

EVENING Times
The Life and Soul of Glasgow
DOUBLE YOUR MONEY TODAY
EXCLUSIVE
OUR STORY
By Scotland's surrogate baby couple
£75,000
SCRATCH FOR CASH
HomeFront
SUPER 12-PAGE PROPERTY PULL-OUT
SCHOOL AXE FURY
21 to close as council tax rockets by 36%
KIDS ATTACKED DURING JACKSON SONG
PULP STAR HELD AT BRITS
BARNUMS

The European newspaper as it appears on the Internet

Objectives

In successfully completing this unit, you will:

1. Talk about the different parts of a newspaper.
2. Talk about how different newspapers present the same story.
3. Write headlines for news stories.
4. Talk about advertisements for a product.
5. Design an advertisement for a similar product.
6. Select and present items for a radio news bulletin.
7. Organise an evening's television and radio entertainment for different viewers/listeners.
8. Compare the way two media present information about drugs.

The Jewish Chronicle. Established in 1841, it is the oldest Jewish newspaper in the world.

ALL THIS WEEK IN YOUR BIG-VALUE MIRROR
GREAT SUMMER THEME PARK DEALS
TODAY KIDS GO FREE AT
WIN DIANA'S DRESS
HENMAN WINS A THRILLER
The Mirror
WE TELL IT LIKE IT IS
30p
BAN BEAST TYSON
EXCLUSIVE: KIDS' TV SOAP IN WAR ON KNIVES: PAGE 5

Introduction

In this unit you are going to talk about newspapers, T.V., radio and advertising. You will think about how these 'mediums' are used to communicate information and how effective they are.

Task

Look at the newspapers on the previous page.

Discuss the elements that make up a newspaper.

How?

During your discussion, you might talk about:

- **A** The different kinds of articles that you would find in a newspaper – for example, world news, local news, gossip.
- **B** Any other types of writing, such as those which do not tell a story. (For example, the T.V. listings page)
- **C** The size and number of illustrations and photographs used in different newspapers.
- **D** The number of pages given to advertisements in different newspapers.
- **E** The sizes of the different newspapers.
- **F** The different types of newspaper, such as national, local, specialist, etc.
- **G** How often the newspapers are published, for example, every day, once a week, etc.

Tips for success

- Make sure you understand the tasks.
- Making notes before the discussion may help you to remember the things you want to talk about.
- Use the How? box to help you through the activity.
- Speak clearly.
- Explain carefully.
- Listen to others.
- Take turns.

The medium of newspapers

In this part of the unit, you will be looking at newspapers. To begin with, you will look at the ways two newspapers write about the same story.

Both newspapers, *The Express* and *The Sun*, report the appearance of ex-Spice Girl Geri Halliwell at London's High Court. The Spice Girls are being sued by Italian firm Aprilia who claim that they are owed over a million pounds by the band.

Task

Read the article *I didn't think I had the power to leave the girls,* which is from *The Express.*

THE EXPRESS, SATURDAY, FEBRUARY 12, 2000

5

GERI TELLS COURT HOW SHE PUT OFF SPICE 'MARRIAGE' SPLIT

By DAVID SMITH

I didn't think I had the power to leave the girls

GERI HALLIWELL felt that walking out on the Spice Girls was "like leaving a marriage," she told the High Court yesterday.

Brushing back blonde waist-length hair, the 27-year-old former Ginger Spice described the turmoil of her split from the girl power band in May, 1998. "What one wants to do and what one does are two different things," she said. "At the back of my mind I wanted to leave but I didn't know whether I was brave enough to leave the security of such a big band.

"So I was drip-feeding the idea to the others and myself to see if I was brave enough. There wasn't one defining moment when I consciously made that decision. It was like leaving a marriage. You get such mixed feelings – one part of me wanted to stay but the other half said it was time to go."

Miss Halliwell, giving evidence in support of her former colleagues in a complex two-way action with the official sponsors of their 1998 world tour, said she had wanted "a little bit of breathing space" before she made new plans.

This was a very different Geri from the strutting Ginger Spice who once raised temperatures in a tight Union Flag dress. Instead, she held a more subtle form of girl power, blinking doe-eyed at cross-examiner Andrew Sutcliffe and answering with smiles of sweet innocence.

After Baby Spice Emma Bunton's confession of a "terrible memory" two days earlier, Miss Halliwell

BREAK-UP: Geri, right, told Posh, left, that she wanted to end with the big finale at Wembley

fared little better as she was forced to reply to numerous questions: "I just can't remember. I really apologise, it was all so long ago."

Yet there was no such lapse when Mr Sutcliffe asked her to recall a newspaper review which hailed the Spice Girls' "dazzling" performance in a concert at the time. After an hour in the witness-box she was whisked away in a blacked-out Mercedes, leaving spokesman Jonathan Hackford to say simply: "I would like to make clear that Geri is not a party to the proceedings. She came voluntarily as a witness to help the girls."

Italian motorcycle manufacturer Aprilia contends that Geri's departure cost it £1.6million in lost profits. The band signed a £500,000 contract with Aprilia to promote its products, including a special Spice Sonic scooter with a picture of all five girls on it.

But the company says that they turned into a "total marketing flop" when Miss Halliwell left. Aprilia claims the group, which is suing the company for £212,000 in unpaid sponsorship and royalties, was aware of Miss Halliwell's plans to quit when they signed the contract. Miss Halliwell, who has since pursued a successful solo career, said she remembered telling the rest of the group on their tour coach in Frankfurt in early March, 1998, that she was thinking of leaving at the end of September.

"I do not think they took me seriously," she explained. She said that later on the tour she "reiterated the fact that I was going to leave." Asked for the band's reaction, she told the court: "I think it was possibly disbelief, a mixed reaction and still not taking it seriously." When Posh Spice Victoria Adams asked why she wanted to leave, she told them that she had had enough and wanted to finish with a big finale at Wembley.

Miss Halliwell said that at one of the band's meetings in April, 1998, it was decided not to immediately release news of her departure. Asked whether that decision was based on the possible adverse impact on the rest of the tour, Miss Halliwell said that it was more "quite an emotional thing among the band." The case continues

Discussing the article

Task

Discuss the article on the previous page with at least one other person.

Record your thoughts in your note book.

How?

Read the article *I didn't think I had the power to leave the girls* from *The Express* and then use these questions to help you discuss it:

A Who is the story about?
B Where did it take place?
C When did the problems start?
D What did Geri say about wanting to leave the band?
E How did Geri tell the band about her decision?
F Why is this story worth reporting?

1. Who ...?
2. Where ...?
3. When ...?
4. What ...?
5. How ...?
6. Why ...?

Tips for success

- Read the article at least twice.
- Make sure you understand the question before you attempt an answer.
- Search the article to make sure you have a full answer.

Comparing the articles

Task

Read the article *Geri: Leaving was like a marriage break-up*, on the opposite page, which is from *The Sun*.

Working with at least one other person, compare it with the article from *The Express* on page 62.

Record your thoughts in your note book.

THE EXPRESS, SATURDAY, FEBRUARY 12, 2000

5

GERI TELLS COURT HOW SHE PUT OFF SPICE 'MARRIAGE' SPLIT

I didn't think I had the power to leave the girls

BREAK-UP: Geri, right, told Posh, left, that she wanted to end with the big finale at Wembley

By DAVID SMITH

GERI HALLIWELL felt that walking out on the Spice Girls was "like leaving a marriage," she told the High Court yesterday.

Brushing back blonde waist-length hair, the 27-year-old former Ginger Spice described the turmoil of her split from the girl power band in May, 1998. "What one [illegible]s to do and what one does are two different things," she said. "At the back of my mind I wanted to leave but I didn't know whether I was brave enough to leave the security of such a big band.

"So I was drip-feeding the idea to the others and myself to see if I was brave enough. There wasn't one defining moment when I consciously made that decision. It was like leaving a marriage. You get such mixed feelings – one part of me wanted to stay but the other half said it was time to go."

Miss Halliwell, giving evidence in support of her former colleagues in a complex two-way action with the official sponsors of their 1998 world tour, said she had wanted "a little bit of breathing space" before she made new plans.

This was a very different Geri from the strutting Ginger Spice who once raised temperatures in a tight Union Flag dress. Instead, she held a more subtle form of girl power, blinking doe-eyed at cross-examiner Andrew Sutcliffe and answering with smiles of sweet innocence.

After Baby Spice Emma Bunton's confession of a "terrible memory" two days earlier, Miss Halliwell fared little better as she was forced to reply to numerous questions: "I just can't remember. I really apologise, it was all so long ago."

Yet there was no such lapse when Mr Sutcliffe asked her to recall a newspaper review which hailed the Spice Girls' "dazzling" performance in a concert at the time. After an hour in the witness-box she was whisked away in a blacked-out Mercedes, leaving spokesman Jonathan Hackford to say simply: "I would like to make clear that Geri is not a party to the proceedings. She came voluntarily as a witness to help the girls."

Italian motorcycle manufacturer Aprilia contends that Geri's departure cost it £1.6million in lost profits. The band signed a £500,000 contract with Aprilia to promote its products, including a special Spice Sonic scooter with a picture of all five girls on it.

But the company says that they turned into a "total marketing flop" when Miss Halliwell left. Aprilia claims the group, which is suing the company for £212,000 in unpaid sponsorship and royalties, was aware of Miss Halliwell's plans to quit when they signed the contract. Miss Halliwell, who has since pursued a successful solo career, said she remembered telling the rest of the group on their tour coach in Frankfurt in early March, 1998, that she was thinking of leaving at the end of September.

"I do not think they took me seriously," she explained. She said that later on the tour she "reiterated the fact that I was going to leave." Asked for the band's reaction, she told the court: "I think it was possibly disbelief, a mixed reaction and still not taking it seriously." When Posh Spice Victoria Adams asked why she wanted to leave, she told them that she had had enough and wanted to finish with a big finale at Wembley.

Miss Halliwell said that at one of the band's meetings in April, 1998, it was decided not to immediately release news of her departure. Asked whether that decision was based on the possible adverse impact on the rest of the tour, Miss Halliwell said that it was more "quite an emotional thing among the band." The case continues

How?

A In order to compare the two articles, you need to think about what things are the same, and what things are different. Note down:
- Five facts which are in both articles.
- Five facts which are mentioned in *The Express* but not in *The Sun*.

B Look at the headlines. Which do you like best? Why?

C Think about which article is the most interesting of the two. Why?

Tips for success

- Read the article *Geri: Leaving was like a marriage break-up* at least twice.
- Re-read the article *I didn't think I had the power to leave the girls*, on page 62.
- Make sure you understand the question before you attempt an answer.
- Search both articles carefully to make sure that you have a full answer.

SPICE COURT BATTLE

THE SUN, Saturday, February 12, 2000 **15**

Geri: Leaving was like a marriage break-up

Girl power ... Geri as Ginger

Witness . . Geri Halliwell leaves court yesterday

By THOMAS WHITAKER

SUPERSTAR singer Geri Halliwell told yesterday how quitting the Spice Girls was like a divorce.

The 27-year-old opened her heart in the High Court where the band is involved in a £1.6million law suit.

Geri – dressed in black and wearing no jewellery – said: "It was like leaving a marriage.

"You get such mixed feelings. One half of you wanted to stay, the other half of you says it's time to go.

"But privately I wanted a bit of breathing space.

"I knew at the back of my mind I wanted to do it. But I didn't know if I was brave enough to do it and leave the security of such a big band."

Geri quit as Ginger Spice in May 1998, during the group's world tour.

Decision

She said: "There was not one deciding moment when I consciously made that decision.

"I was drip-feeding the idea to them and myself."

Geri was appearing as a witness for Spice Girls Limited, who are being sued for £1.6million by Italian scooter firm Aprilia.

Bosses claim that is what they lost by making a bike featuring pictures of five Spice Girls – and insist they would have scrapped the idea if they had known Geri was poised to quit.

At the same time the band are suing the firm for £212,000 which they say is still owed from their £500,000 deal.

Geri was criticised by Aprilia's barrister Andrew Sutcliffe for not warning the firm about her plans.

He said Aprilia should have been made aware she had threatened on three occasions to quit before the deal was signed. During a one-hour examination, Mr Sutcliffe asked: "Did it concern you Aprilia might produce a scooter showing five of you when you knew you were going? Did it not occur to you to tell your main sponsor of your decision?"

Geri: "I felt the Spice Girls were strong enough and had a momentum to go on as a four-piece even though I was leaving."

Mr Sutcliffe: "Were you not worried about young Italian girls buying a scooter promoted with faces of the five of you on it?"

Geri: "I think that is down to opinion. I can't speak for a young Italian girl."

The court heard Geri, who finally quit on May 31, told the band about her plans to leave three times before the Aprilia deal was signed on May 6.

She said the first time was on March 3 in Frankfurt, Germany.

Geri told Judge Mrs Justice Arden: "I didn't think they took me seriously."

The second time was six days later before a gig in Milan.

Geri said of the girls' reaction: "It was possibly disbelief and a mixed reaction and they were still not taking me seriously." The third time was a meeting with the girls and lawyer Andrew Thompson on April 25. Mr Sutcliffe said Aprilia should have been informed after that because her decision to quit made the "Spice-sonic" scooter obsolete.

Geri said: "There were a lot of reasons why this was not announced. It was quite an emotional thing for the band. We wanted our own privacy and to come to terms with it first.

"We were also doing lots of other things and telling them (Aprilia) didn't cross my mind."

Important

Earlier, Paul Morrison, who negotiated the Aprilia deal, said he was unaware Geri was leaving when the contract was signed.

The judge asked if it was important Aprilia knew of Geri's plans.

Mr Morrison replied: "It was very important."

The judge then asked: "If you knew Geri was leaving, would you have said anything to Aprilia?" Mr Morrison said: "Yes, unless we were told not to."

Baby Spice Emma Bunton, 24, has already given evidence. The hearing is set to end next week.

Is Geri turning into Madonna?
– see Pages 34–35

Headlines

Headlines are words or phrases that appear at the top of a newspaper article. Headlines are meant to:

- Catch the reader's attention.
- Make the reader want to read the article.
- Tell the reader a little bit about what the article is about.

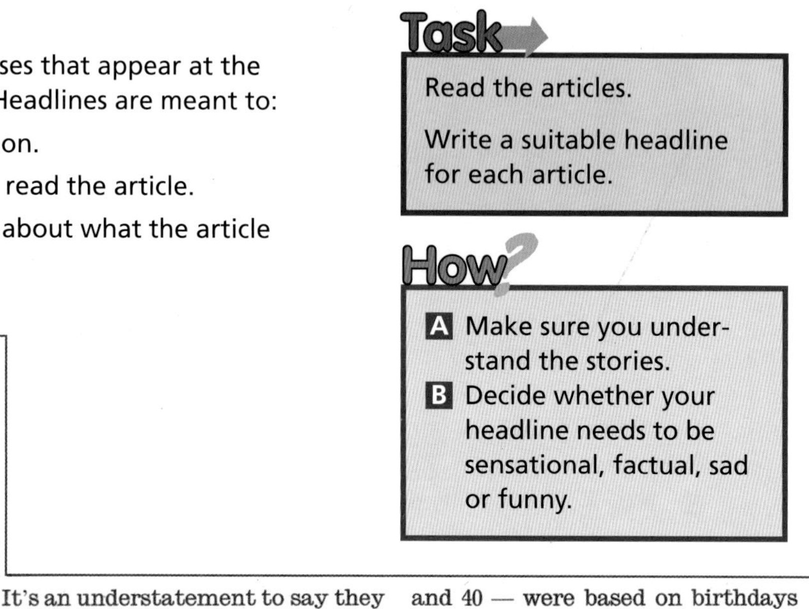

Task

Read the articles.

Write a suitable headline for each article.

How?

A Make sure you understand the stories.

B Decide whether your headline needs to be sensational, factual, sad or funny.

EXCLUSIVE

By BILL DANIELS

PIE salesman Sean Taylor was celebrating last night after winning the £9.5 million Lottery jackpot.

The ecstatic father of three woke neighbours in the early hours to tell them of his good fortune.

Then Sean, 31, and his hairdresser wife Alex started partying at their home in Coalville, Leics.

One neighbour said: "They could not contain themselves. They got us out of bed at 2am to tell us.

"They were totally stunned and were finding it difficult to take in.

"They just wanted someone to share the happy news with them. It's an understatement to say they were thrilled." She added: "Sean and Alex are a lovely couple with wonderful children.

"It could not have happened to a nicer family."

Sean, who used to have a market stall in Leicester, works as a rep for a company in Loughborough.

He is a keen amateur soccer player and Leicester City fan. His winning numbers — 6, 20, 29, 31, 35 and 40 — were based on birthdays and ages in his family.

Last night the couple and their children — two boys and a girl, aged two to seven — were in hiding after leaving their home.

A neighbour said: "They have had lots of visitors — all their family.

"They decided in the end to get away for a bit of peace and quiet.

"It is going to take them some time to come to terms with it."

By LOUISE THOMAS

LOCAL COUNCILLORS were today presented with a petition to improve road safety around the notorious Blackmore Heath High Road. The petition, signed by over 5,000 residents, was presented to the council by Mrs Jean McLucas, whose son, Brian, was killed on the road two weeks ago.

Mrs McLucas was devastated when 11 year-old Brian was hit by a car and killed, while on his way to scout camp. However, she is determined not to let his death be in vain. She is campaigning to have a zebra crossing added to the road. Mrs McLucas, of Wheltands Lane, said: "All the mums know how dangerous the road is. We have asked the council again and again to do something, but they say that they just don't have the money. No matter how careful the kids are, there are always going to be accidents, unless there's a safe place to cross. There should always be money available if it saves lives."

Councillor Elliot Brown said: "This is not the first time that this road has claimed a life, and we will certainly be looking at ways of improving safety. However, any decision will depend on how much money there is in the budget at the end of the year."

The medium of advertising

In this part of the unit, you are going to look at the ways in which different products are advertised by different companies.

You will then design an advertisement of your own.

Selling perfume

Task

Look at the advertisement for Charlie Sunshine.

Talk about it with at least one other person.

How?

Use these questions to help you to talk about the advertisement. Think about the words:

A Are we told that Charlie Sunshine is a new product?

B What do the phrases "get up!" and "feel that sunshine" suggest to you about the perfume?

C Why does each phrase have an exclamation mark?

D What do the words suggest about the sort of person who might use the product?

Think about the picture:

A What kind of a person does the girl seem to be? (Look at her hair, her eyes, her expression, the way she is standing, her clothing.)

B Why do you think the products are so close to the model?

C The background colour reflects the name of the product. What other reasons might there be for choosing a golden background?

Think about what kind of people the advertisement is trying to attract.

Tips for success

- Make sure you understand the tasks.
- Making notes before the discussion may help you to remember the things you want to talk about.
- Use the How? box to help you through the activity.
- Speak clearly.
- Explain carefully.
- Listen to others.
- Take turns.

SELL!

Selling a fragrance

Task

Look at the advertisement for Paco.

Talk about it with at least one other person.

How?

Use these questions to help you to talk about the advertisement.

Think about the words:

A Why do you think the product is called Paco?

B Why does the advertisement say that the can is "aluminium" and "recyclable"?

C Why does the advertisement say that the product is "for every-one on the planet"?

D Why does the advertisement say so little about the smell of Paco?

The picture:

A Why is the can the only picture on the advertisement?

B The layout is very simple – a picture of the can and some print. Do you think that this is a good idea? Why?

C This advertisement is black and white. Do you think this is a good idea? Why?

it's aluminium it's recyclable it's for men it's for women it's for me it's for you it's for everyone on the planet and it smells good.*

* of course it does it's a fragrance.

Comparing the advertisements

Research

Find at least two more advertisements for perfume or aftershave.

Task

Look again at all four advertisements.

With at least one other person, talk about how they compare.

How?

Talk about:

A The words used and what image they give to the product. For example, do they make it seem exciting or glamorous?

B The pictures used.

C The types of people the advertisements are trying to attract to the product.

D Which advertisement you like best and why.

E Which advertisement you like least and why.

Tips for success

- Make sure you understand the tasks.
- Think again of what you talked about when you looked at the advertisements for Charlie Sunshine and Paco.
- Making notes before the discussion may help you to remember the things you want to talk about.
- Use the How? box to help you through the activity.
- Speak clearly.
- Explain carefully.
- Listen to others.
- Take turns.

Your turn

Task

Design an advertisement for a new perfume or aftershave.

How?

Before designing your advertisement, think about the following questions:

- **A** Is your product for men or women?
- **B** What age group is it intended for?
- **C** What will attract buyers to your product (for example, famous label, expensive, refreshing, etc.)?
- **D** What are you going to call your product?
- **E** What does the name suggest about your product?
- **F** What words or information will you use to persuade people to buy it?
- **G** What sort of pictures will you use?
- **H** What colours will you use?
- **I** Will the product be shown in the advertisement? If you answer yes, where will it be?

Tips for success

- Try out some of your ideas on paper. Try different positions for words and pictures. For the first draft, you need only draw quick sketches of your ideas.
- Decide which idea you like best and produce a finished version of your advertisement.
- Take great care with your final presentation.
- Write neatly.
- Draw and colour the advertisement carefully.

ERASER

The medium of radio

In this exercise you are going to put yourself in the place of a team of radio producers. Every hour, most radio stations have a news bulletin. During the bulletin, they have to:

- Present whatever news they have for the day.
- Decide how long to give each item.
- Decide how much information to give.

Most radio stations have a set time for the news, and a regular way of presenting it, called a format. Most news broadcasts follow a similar pattern:

- The news begins with the theme tune.
- The radio announcer then introduces the news, gives the time, and introduces himself or herself.
- The announcer reads out the headlines of the most important stories.
- The news begins with the most important story and then moves onto the stories that were headlined.
- The bulletin ends with an unusual or lighthearted story.
- The announcer tells the audience the time of the next broadcast.

The script may look like this:

NEWS BULLETIN NEWS BULLETIN NEWS BULLETIN
14.00 City Radio Thur. Jul. 12th 1998

GOOD AFTERNOON. MY NAME IS KEVIN O'DOCHERTY AND THIS IS THE NEWS AT 2 O'CLOCK.

DUR: 8"

THE GOVERNMENT TODAY ANNOUNCED PLANS TO USE LOTTERY MONEY TO BOOST EDUCATION AND HEALTH SERVICES.

THE PROPOSALS AIM TO MAKE A SUBSTANTIAL PORTION OF LOTTERY MONEY AVAILABLE TO EDUCATION AND HEALTH AUTHORITIES THROUGHOUT BRITAIN.

DUR: 22"
TIME: 30"

THE HOME SECRETARY'S NEW ANTI-RACIST BILL RECEIVED ITS FIRST READING IN THE COMMONS TODAY.

COMMUNITY LEADERS HAILED THE BILL AS A GREAT STEP FORWARD IN RACE RELATIONS.

DUR: 20"
TOTAL: 50"

NEW BOY BAND *SHORT CUT* TODAY ANNOUNCED DETAILS OF THEIR LONG-AWAITED TOUR.

NO DETAILS ARE AVAILABLE AS YET.

DUR: 12"
TOTAL: 62"

ACTOR BRIAN COLINIEW DIED TODAY AT HIS SOUTHPORT HOME. HE HAD BEEN ILL FOR SOME TIME.

FRIENDS TODAY GATHERED TO PAY TRIBUTE TO SOMEONE WHO HAD BECOME A HOUSEHOLD NAME DURING HIS 46 YEARS IN SHOW BUSINESS.

DUR: 27"
TOTAL: 89"

AND FINALLY A PORTSMOUTH HOUSEWIFE WAS TODAY CELEBRATING THE BIRTH OF HER FIRST DAUGHTER.

THE 36-YEAR-OLD MOTHER OF TWELVE WAS SAID TO BE DELIGHTED BUT NOT PLANNING ANY MORE CHILDREN FOR A WHILE.

DUR: 18"
TOTAL: 107"

AND THOSE ARE TODAYS MAIN HEADLINES. JOIN US FOR ANOTHER CITY RADIO BULLETIN AT 4.

DUR: 5"
TIME: 120"

Preparing your news script

You are going to read a selection of news articles and use the information in them to prepare a radio news script.

Task

Read the newspaper articles with at least one other person.

A

Two killed in blaze horror

A TEENAGER and a baby died when fire swept through a flat yesterday.

A man and another child were seriously injured after they jumped 25ft from an upstairs window.

The baby girl was found dead in the flat above an Indian restaurant in Sunderland, Tyne and Wear.

The teenage girl died when she plunged from a second-floor window.

A woman and a third child fled unhurt.

B

RINGO'S HOME IS STARR ATTRACTION

THE rundown terrace house in Liverpool where Beatles drummer Ringo Starr was born may be given historic status as a listed building.

That's the aim of new owner Cliff Cooper who bought No.9 Madryn Street, Toxteth, for £13,200 at an auction in March.

English Heritage said any application would be considered "very seriously". The National Trust has already bought Sir Paul McCartney's childhood home. But Ringo's house would be the first birthplace of a living person to be listed.

Owner Cliff, head of World of Music shops, admitted it was "in a terrible state", with a shaky roof and ceilings.

C

Tape books all the rage

TAPED versions of books and TV comedy shows are selling in millions, thanks to car jams and road rage.

Many motorists find the spoken word more soothing than music.

Now the tape trade is worth £50million a year – four times the figure of five years ago, a survey revealed yesterday.

Books make up 40 per cent, TV and radio 25. Language tapes and children's stories also sell well.

D

DRIVERS CALL FOR ROAD RAGE LAWS

NEARLY all motorists think road rage should be made an offence.

Ninety three per cent of car users want new laws to punish aggressive drivers. Almost the same number believe driving is more stressful than it was a decade ago.

An RAC and Auto Express magazine survey out yesterday revealed 600,000 drivers have been punched and attacked on the road and more than a million have been rammed by another car.

The RAC's Richard Woods said: "This survey confirms motorists' concerns over aggression and stress on our roads.

"We can all help by choosing courtesy instead of confrontation when driving."

E

Man charged with abduction

A MAN accused of the abduction of a 17-year-old girl from Gatley was remanded in custody by magistrates this week.

Nicholas Burton, aged 27, is charged with kidnapping, falsely imprisoning and threatening to kill Deborah Van Gerko, who is an A-level student at Cheadle's Ridge Danyer's College, on Saturday, April 26. He was arrested at a hotel in Bangor, North Wales.

Balding and dressed in a black waistcoat and black polo neck shirt, Mr Burton, from New Mills, appeared before Stockport magistrates on Wednesday.

He was handcuffed and was flanked by two guards during the hearing.

He told the justices he was not represented by a solicitor.

The hearing was delayed for an hour while he spoke to a duty solicitor and when the court resumed Mr Burton remained unrepresented.

The magistrates remanded him in custody until today, Friday, May 2.

Recording your bulletin

Task

Prepare a two-minute news script.

Record your news script.

How?

- **A** Look again at the newspaper articles on the previous page.
- **B** Put them in order, so that the most important comes first.
- **C** Each of the articles will be an item in your news bulletin. Decide on what information from the article that you want to include for each item.
- **D** Give each of your items a headline.
- **E** Set out your script as shown on page 72.
- **F** Read your script through and time your reading.
- **G** Make changes to ensure that your script lasts for only two minutes.
- **H** Practise reading your script over several times.
- **I** Record it once, play it back and listen to it.
- **J** If you are not satisfied, record it again.

Tips for success

- Re-read all of the articles.
- Make careful notes.
- When recording your bulletin speak clearly and slowly.
- Avoid long pauses between items.

The medium of television

You will be very familiar with T.V. pages in newspapers and magazines. They have two main elements.

- Information about the programmes to be shown on a particular day and the time these programmes begin.
- Opinions of some of the programmes that appear on our screens.

In this unit you will work with both of these types of material.

Task

Look at the T.V. listings page, below.

BBC1

6.00 BUSINESS BREAKFAST
7.00 NEWS 9.00 Breakfast Extra News **9.20** Style Challenge **9.45** Kilroy **10.30** Can't Cook, Won't Cook **11.00** News; Weather **11.05** The Great Escape **11.35** Change That
12.00 NEWS 12.05 Call My Bluff **12.35** Good Living
1.00 NEWS WEATHER 1.30 Regional News; Weather **1.40** The Weather Show
1.45 NEIGHBOURS 2.10 Quincy **2.55** Through the Keyhole **3.20** A Perfect Arrangement
3.30 CHILDREN'S BBC: Playdays **3.50** Postman Pat **4.05** Felix the Cat **4.20** Julia Jekyl and Harriet Hyde **4.35** Return to Jupiter **5.00** Newsround **5.10** No Sweat
5.35 NEIGHBOURS
6.00 NEWS; WEATHER
6.30 REGIONAL NEWS
7.00 WATCHDOG Consumer affairs
7.30 EASTENDERS Soap
8.00 ANIMAL HOSPITAL
8.30 KEEPING MUM Sitcom
9.00 NEWS; WEATHER
9.30 999 Real life drama
10.20 MATCH OF THE DAY
11.00 QUESTION TIME Topical discussion
12.05 FILM: THE ODD COUPLE (1967) Comedy
1.45 WEATHER
1.55 CLOSE

BBC2

6.00 OPEN UNIVERSITY 7.15 See Hear Breakfast News **7.30** Teenage Mutant Hero Turtles **7.55** Blue Peter **8.20** Fireman Sam **8.35** Racoons **9.00** Daytime on Two **10.00** Teletubbies **10.30** Daytime on Two
12.30 WORKING LUNCH 1.00 Lifeschool **1.25** Science in Action **1.45** Numbertime **2.00** Fireman Sam
2.10 GOLF
6.00 STAR TREK: DEEP SPACE NINE Sci-fi
6.45 QUANTUM LEAP Sci-fi
7.30 EAST Asian current affairs
8.00 OUT AND ABOUT Nature documentary
8.30 TOP GEAR
9.00 ABSOLUTELY FABULOUS Comedy
9.30 THIS LIFE Soap
10.30 NEWSNIGHT
11.00 LATE REVIEW Film reviews
11.55 THE PHIL SILVERS SHOW Classic comedy

CHANNEL 4

6.00 SESAME STREET 7.00 The Big Breakfast **9.00** Bewitched **9.30** Those British faces
10.00 FILM: CHAMPAGNE CHARLIE (1944) Comedy
11.55 PENCIL DANCE 12.00 Australia Wild **12.30** Light Lunch **1.30** Waterways
2.00 RACING
4.00 FIFTEEN TO ONE Quiz
4.30 COUNTDOWN Quiz
5.00 RICKI LAKE Chat
5.30 PET RESCUE
6.00 FRIENDS Sitcom
6.25 FLUKE
7.00 NEWS; WEATHER
8.00 MOVING PEOPLE Documentary
8.30 BROOKSIDE
9.00 THE INVESTIGATOR Real-life drama
10.45 FILM: FOOL FOR LOVE (1985) Romance
12.40 FILM: WESTWORLD (1973) Sci-fi
2.35 FILM: THE PLAGUE OF THE ZOMBIES (1965) Horror
4.15 FLIGHT OF THE SWAN 4.30 Raiders of the Dawn **5.30** Backdate

ITV

GMTV 9.25 Supermarket Sweep **9.55** Regional News **10.00** The Time...The Place **10.30** This Morning **12.20** Regional News **12.30** News; Weather **12.25** Shortland Street
1.25 HOME AND AWAY Soap
1.50 AFTERNOON LIVE
2.20 VANESSA Chat
2.50 AFTERNOON LIVE
3.20 NEWS
3.25 REGIONAL NEWS
3.30 CHILDREN'S ITV: Wizadora **3.40** Potamus Park **3.50** Bimble's Bucket **4.00** Garfield and Friends **4.15** Hey Arnold! **4.40** Island
5.10 HOME AND AWAY
5.40 NEWS; WEATHER
6.00 REGIONAL NEWS
6.30 JENNY'S COUNTRY COOKING
7.00 EMMERDALE Soap
7.30 WHO PUT THE BEAT IN MERSEY BEAT? Music documentary
8.00 THE BILL Police drama
8.30 THE COOK REPORT
9.00 TOUCHING EVIL Drama
10.00 NEWS; WEATHER
10.30 REGIONAL NEWS
10.40 NETWORK FIRST Documentary
11.40 EMMERDALE 12.40 Collins and Maconie's Movie Club
1.15 FILM: UNDERCOVER BLUES (1993) Comedy crime busting
2.55 IN FOCUS 3.40 Nationwide Football League Extra **4.30** Curtis Calls **4.45** cyber.cafe **5.00** The Time...The Place **5.30** News

CHANNEL 5

6.00 NEWS **7.30** Havakazoo **8.00** Adventures of the Bush Patrol **8.30** Wideworld **9.00** Expresso **10.00** Exclusive **10.30** Hot Property **11.00** Leeza **11.50** Double Expresso
12.00 THE BOLD AND THE BEAUTIFUL
12.30 FAMILY AFFAIRS Soap
1.00 NEWS
1.05 SUNSET BEACH Soap
2.00 5's COMPANY – LATE EXTRA
3.30 FILM: THE SECRET LIFE OF CATHY McCORMICK (1988) Drama
5.20 5's COMPANY - LATE EXTRA
5.30 100 PERCENT Quiz
6.00 WHITTLE Quiz
6.30 FAMILY AFFAIRS Soap
7.00 EXCLUSIVE Entertainment news
7.30 WILD STATES Nature documentary
8.00 FAME AND FORTUNE Documentary
8.30 NEWS
9.00 FILM: RED DAWN (1984) Action adventure
11.00 THE JACK DOCHERTY SHOW Chat
11.40 THE COMEDY STORE
12.10 LIVE AND DANGEROUS 4.00 Prisoner Cell Block H **5.40** 100 Percent

At home ...

In many homes, a person might have to agree to let someone else watch or listen to one programme so that he or she can watch another programme without arguments. However, if you had the T.V. to yourself for an evening, what would you choose to watch?

Task

Choose an entertaining evening's viewing and listening for yourself, using the listings page.

Choose the T.V. evening from Hell for an enemy.

Choose an evening's entertainment for your whole family. Make sure you choose something to please each member of your family.

Write down your three lists.

How?

A Decide on your favourite and least favourite types of programme.

B Look at all the T.V. programmes.

C Make a note of correct times and channels.

D Write one sentence stating what you know about each programme.

Tips for success

- Read the listings carefully.
- Try to get a balance of programmes – something for everyone.

Be a critic

Most newspapers employ someone to watch programmes and write opinions about them. This person is called a T.V. critic and will often be allowed to watch programmes before they appear on our television screens. Here is one critic's review of a new comedy series and several other programmes.

SARKY and sassy, Emma Wray is back, shooting from the lip, as a lass in blunderland in Simon Nye's new comedy drama *My Wonderful Life* (ITV, Thursday).

Predictably, Wray's a laugh as Donna, a single-parent nurse with attitude problems spouting wry, dry Nye lines like "I was delayed by an imploding artificial hip" and declaring she only became a nurse because "I was too short to be Home Secretary".

Nye, of course, delivered the smash hit *Men Behaving Badly*, and Emma received multiple hoo-Wrays for her perky performance in seven series of *Watching*.

Too early to expect the new show to jump, like Barnsley FC, right into the big time.

But former gymnast Emma always has bounce – and showed many of her Mersey qualities as a girl behaving badly, splurging £200 baby-sitting money on a night of booze, darts and a grope in the back of an ambulance.

Familiar faces in support too: ex-Minder Gary Webster as a paramedic with a gruesome line of chat about severed heads and Tony Robinson, a gem again as a patronising neighbour.

Watch too for shameless scene-stealing from Donna's bolshie brood Rhiannon (Amanda Riley), and Shirley (Vicky Connett), who is lined up for an hilarious appearance down the run in her first Holy Communion gown and baseball boots! My Wonderful Life isn't Nye on top form. Yet.

But it has a Wray of hope.

● DINGLE bile from Uncle Albert (Bobby Knutt and sweet as one in the part) recalling his wife on his wedding day at Eric Pollard's stag night in *Emmerdale*.

"She had corned beef legs and weighed 23 stones – one for every year," he recalled.

Task

Read the reviews.

Watch a T.V. programme.

Write your own review of that programme.

How?

A Read the articles carefully before writing your own review.

B Look at how Lanning includes the following details in his review:

- The name of the programme.
- The type of programme it is, for example, comedy, drama, soap.
- The names of the writer and main actors.
- Any other interesting information about the actors' other programmes.
- His opinion of the programme.

QUICK TAKES

● SO Tricia Armstrong, whose love life always ended up going through Fred Elliott's mincer, said cheerio, chuck in *Corrie*.

A pity she's taking son Jamie, whom Joseph Gilgun has made into one of the most delightfully deadpan, dead-end kids on the box.

He should return, if only to feed Jack Duckworth's pigeons. He's always had lofty ambitions with them.

● HEAVEN knows, anything must go if GMTV's totally unattainable Penny Smith can display more than just a glimpse of stocking.

Normally, as starchly correct as Eric Cantona's collar, she appeared in a pleated, white micro pelmet for her tennis session with Tim Henman.

And not since the breathtaking day when Angela Rippon flashed her knickers and went high-kicking with Morecambe and Wise has there been so many sighs over thighs.

Ruthless Henman still ran her ragged all over the court, leaving the Penny well spent.

● O HENRY! Most of Lenny's links on *The BAFTA Awards* (BBC1, Tuesday) were more NAFF-TA than BAFTA. Even Diana Ross's hair turned purple after his impression of her singing was less than Supreme.

Tips for success

- Make notes or, if possible, video the T.V. programme that you want to review.
- Check your facts carefully before you begin writing.
- Use the How? box to help you through the activity.

Media – dealing with an issue

L.S.D.

know the score

You can get flashbacks. These can happen at any time, and even if the original trip was O.K. the flashback could be a nightmare.

Taking L.S.D. can make you panic and even lead to a permanent change of personality.

The effects of an L.S.D. trip can last for up to 12 hours and that's going to make it difficult avoiding your parents. It could also be a complete nightmare if it's a bad trip. Once the trip has started, it can't be stopped.

Take L.S.D. and you could start seeing things that you don't want to see.

Taking L.S.D. could make you feel sick and throw up. This can be really frightening when you're tripping.

The strengths of trips can vary a lot. There's no way of knowing how much you're taking or what effect it'll have.

Task

Look at the poster about L.S.D.

Talk about it with at least one other person.

How?

Use these questions to help you to talk about the poster. Think about the words:

A Why do you think the words "know the score" have been included?

B Which two of the warnings do you think are the most important? Why?

Think about the picture:

A Why do you think the girl's face is shown as it is?

B Do you think this method works well or not?

Think about the audience:

A Who do you think the poster is aimed at? Why?

SPEED

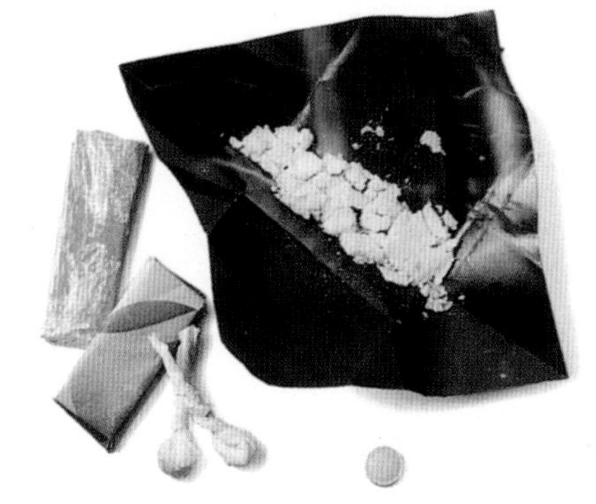

SPEED or amphetamine has been around since the 1930's and was once commonly prescribed by doctors. Now however, it is a very different story as we know more about the harmful side effects of taking Speed. Sometimes called Whizz or Uppers, Speed comes in lots of different forms. Most commonly it comes as a white powder contained in a 'wrap' which is a small folded piece of paper that looks a bit like a small envelope. It is mainly sold in clubs amongst friends or by dealers. Like Ecstasy, Speed increases confidence, sociability and energy levels. It costs £10-£15 for a gramme and is usually swallowed, or sniffed up the nose, or occasionally injected. Speed takes about half an hour to work, depending on its purity and the user's tolerance. The effects usually last for several hours with the user feeling hyperactive, happy and wide awake. Speed is addictive and illegal when not prescribed.

Task

Read the article about Speed.

Look again at the poster about L.S.D.

With at least one other person, talk about how they compare.

How?

Use these questions to help you to compare the article with the poster:

A Who do you think the article is aimed at? Why do you think this is?

B Which of the two items gives you the most useful information?

C Which is easier to follow? Why?

D Which do you like best?

E From looking at the article and poster, which of the drugs do you think is the most dangerous? Why?

Tips for success

- Think again of what you talked about when you looked at the advertisements for Charlie Sunshine and Paco.

Legends and mysteries

Objectives

In successfully completing this unit, you will:

1. Read about and discuss the Bermuda Triangle.
2. Listen to *The Legend of Alderley* and talk about it.
3. Plan and complete a piece of personal writing based on *The Legend of Alderley* or the Bermuda Triangle.
4. Carry out some research into a legend or mystery.
5. Compare your legend or mystery with either *The Legend of Alderley* or the Bermuda Triangle.

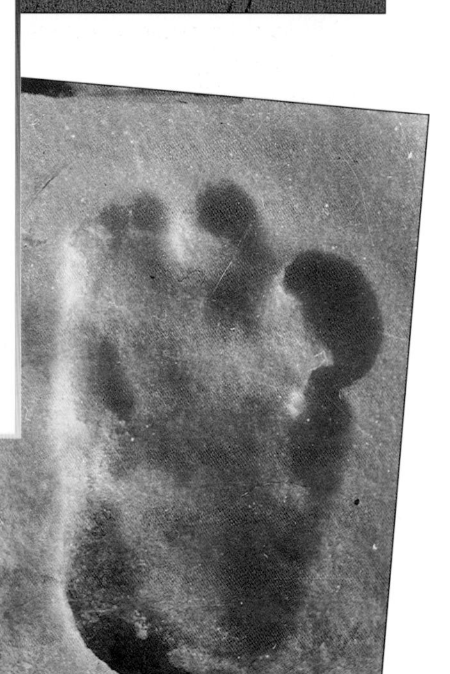

Introduction

In this unit you are going to read about and discuss the mystery of the Bermuda Triangle and *The Legend of Alderley*. You will then complete a piece of writing based on either the Bermuda Triangle or *The Legend of Alderley*.

Task

Look at the pictures on the previous page.

Discuss the legends and mysteries shown with at least one other person.

EXCALIBVR RETURNS TO THE MERE

How?

During your discussion, you might talk about:

A Which legends and mysteries you recognise. (Describe what you know about each one.)

B Which of the legends and mysteries shown you believe in, and why.

C Which other legends or mysteries you know about. (Talk about them.)

Tips for success

- Make sure you understand the tasks.
- Making notes before the discussion may help you to remember the things you want to talk about.
- Use the How? box to help you through the activity.
- Speak clearly.
- Explain carefully.
- Listen to others.
- Take turns.

The Bermuda Triangle

The Bermuda Triangle is a large area, mainly sea, which lies between Puerto Rico, Bermuda and Florida. For over 500 years, many people have been convinced that there is something very odd about the area. Many aeroplanes and ships have disappeared there without any wreckage or bodies being found. A selection of stories, set out here, give a flavour of the mystery:

1492 Christopher Columbus, on his famous journey to discover America, described how he saw a fireball landing in the sea and an unusual glow on the horizon. At the same time his compass stopped working.

1609 The Sea Venture, a British sailing boat, was wrecked off the coast of Bermuda. The night before, sailors saw a very bright, star-like light moving from sail to sail on the ship. It was visible most of the night.

1945 Five U.S. bombers set off from Florida to patrol the Atlantic. The weather was fine and clear. Suddenly an emergency radio message was received stating that the radar had failed and the flight had lost its course. Then radio contact began to break up. A rescue team consisting of thirteen people was sent out. Neither the five bombers nor the rescue team were ever seen again.

1955 A look-out on the Atlantic City saw a large ball of fire passing overhead. At the same time, the compass and the electronic steering failed and the ship began to go round in circles.

1964 A pilot flying to Florida suddenly spotted a strange glow around the wings of his aeroplane. The light became brighter and brighter until his electronic equipment failed and he was left to fly without any instruments to help him. Eventually the light began to fade and his electronic instruments began to work properly once more.

1974 The QE2, a cruise liner, was sailing through the Bermuda Triangle, when all the boilers suddenly stopped working and there was a massive electrical and mechanical failure. At the same time, a local coast-guard boat, which was following the QE2 on its radar, reported that the ship totally disappeared from its radar screens during this time.

Is there a reasonable explanation for these mysterious happenings? Several theories have been suggested. Some say that all of the incidents can be explained by sudden storms, fast-moving currents, or by the pirates who attack and steal small boats for drug smuggling in that area. However, some more unusual reasons are also suggested. Some believe aliens are studying our planet and have taken 'specimens' from the Bermuda Triangle. Others believe that the disturbances are caused by activity in the Earth's crust which leads to earthquakes and whirlpools. They also believe that bursts of magnetic activity in the Earth's molten iron core can explain the frequent reports of spinning compasses and the breakdown of electronic equipment.

However, the fact is that no-one really knows for sure.

Task

Use the information you have just read to answer these questions:

1. Where is the Bermuda Triangle?
2. Why does it have a strange reputation?
3. Pick out any similarities between the incidents you have read.
4. Find five reasons that people use to explain the strange events in the Bermuda Triangle.
5. In your opinion, which is the best explanation? Give reasons.

The Legend of Alderley

In Cheshire there is a local beauty spot called Alderley Edge. Local people tell the story of the wizard Merlin and the knights he has gathered together in a cavern underneath Alderley Edge – ready to rescue England when the country faces danger.

At dawn one still October day in the long ago of the world, across the hill of Alderley, a farmer from Mobberley was riding to Macclesfield fair.

The morning was dull, but mild; light mists bedimmed his way; the woods were hushed; the day promised fine. The farmer was in good spirits, and he let his horse, a milk-white mare, set her own pace, for he wanted her to arrive fresh for the market. A rich man would walk back to Mobberley that night.

So, his mind in the town while he was yet on the hill, the farmer drew near to the place known as Thieves' Hole. And there the horse stood still and would answer neither spur or rein ... In the middle of the path, where surely there had been no one, was an old man, tall, with long hair and beard.

'You go to market to sell this mare,' he said. 'I come here to buy. What is your price?'

But the farmer wished only to sell at the market, where he could have the choice of many offers, so he rudely bade the stranger quit the path and let him through, for if he stayed longer he would be late to the fair.

'Then go your way,' said the old man. 'None will buy. And I shall await you here at sunset.'

The next moment he was gone, and the farmer could not tell how or where.

The day was warm, and the tavern cool, and all who saw the mare agreed that she was a splendid animal ... but no one offered to buy. A sour-eyed farmer rode out of Macclesfield at the end of the day.

Near Thieves' Hole the mare stopped: the stranger was there. Thinking any price was now better than none, the farmer agreed to sell.

'How much will you give?' he said.

'Enough. Now come with me.'

By Seven Firs and Goldenstone they went, to Stormy Point and Saddlebole. And they halted before a great rock embedded in the hillside. The old man lifted his staff and lightly touched the rock, and it split asunder with the noise of thunder ... The wizard, for such he was ... said 'Do not be afraid: for living wonders you shall see here.'

Beyond the rock stood a pair of iron gates. These the wizard opened, and took the farmer and his horse down a narrow tunnel deep into the hill ... The passage ended, and they stepped into a cave, and there a wondrous sight met the farmer's eyes – a hundred and forty knights in silver armour, and by the side of all but one a milky-white mare.

'Here they lie in enchanted sleep,' said the wizard, 'until a day will come – and come it will – when England shall be in direst peril, and England's mother weep. Then out from the hill these must ride and, in battle thrice lost, thrice won, upon a plain, drive the enemy into the sea.'

The farmer, dumb with awe, turned with the wizard into a further cavern, and here mounds of gold and silver and precious stones lay strewn along the ground.

'Take what you can carry in payment for the horse.' And when the farmer had crammed his pockets ... the wizard hurled him up the long tunnel and thrust him out of the gates. The farmer stumbled, the thunder rolled, he looked, and there was only the rock above him. He was alone on the hill, near Stormy Point. The broad moon was up, and it was night.

Task

Read *The Legend of Alderley.*

Answer the following:

1. When did the story take place?
2. Where was the farmer going?
3. What happened to the horse when it reached Thieves' Hole?
4. Why did the farmer refuse to sell his horse to the old man at first?
5. Why did he agree to sell the horse on his way home?
6. What did the farmer see in the cavern?
7. How was he paid for his horse?
8. Which parts of the story suggest to you that it is not true?

Your turn

Now that you have read *The Legend of Alderley* and the information about the Bermuda Triangle, you are going to use what you have learnt about one of them in a piece of writing.

Task

Plan and produce a piece of writing based on *The Legend of Alderley* or the mystery of the Bermuda Triangle.

Choose at least one of the following:

Imagine that you are the farmer in the story *The Legend of Alderley*. Write about what happened to you on the day you met the wizard.

Make a comic strip version of *The Legend of Alderley*.

Imagine that you have just returned from a boat trip in the Bermuda Triangle during which something unusual happened. You have been asked to appear on a radio programme to tell your story. Write the conversation that takes place with the interviewer. Set out your work as a radio script.

How?

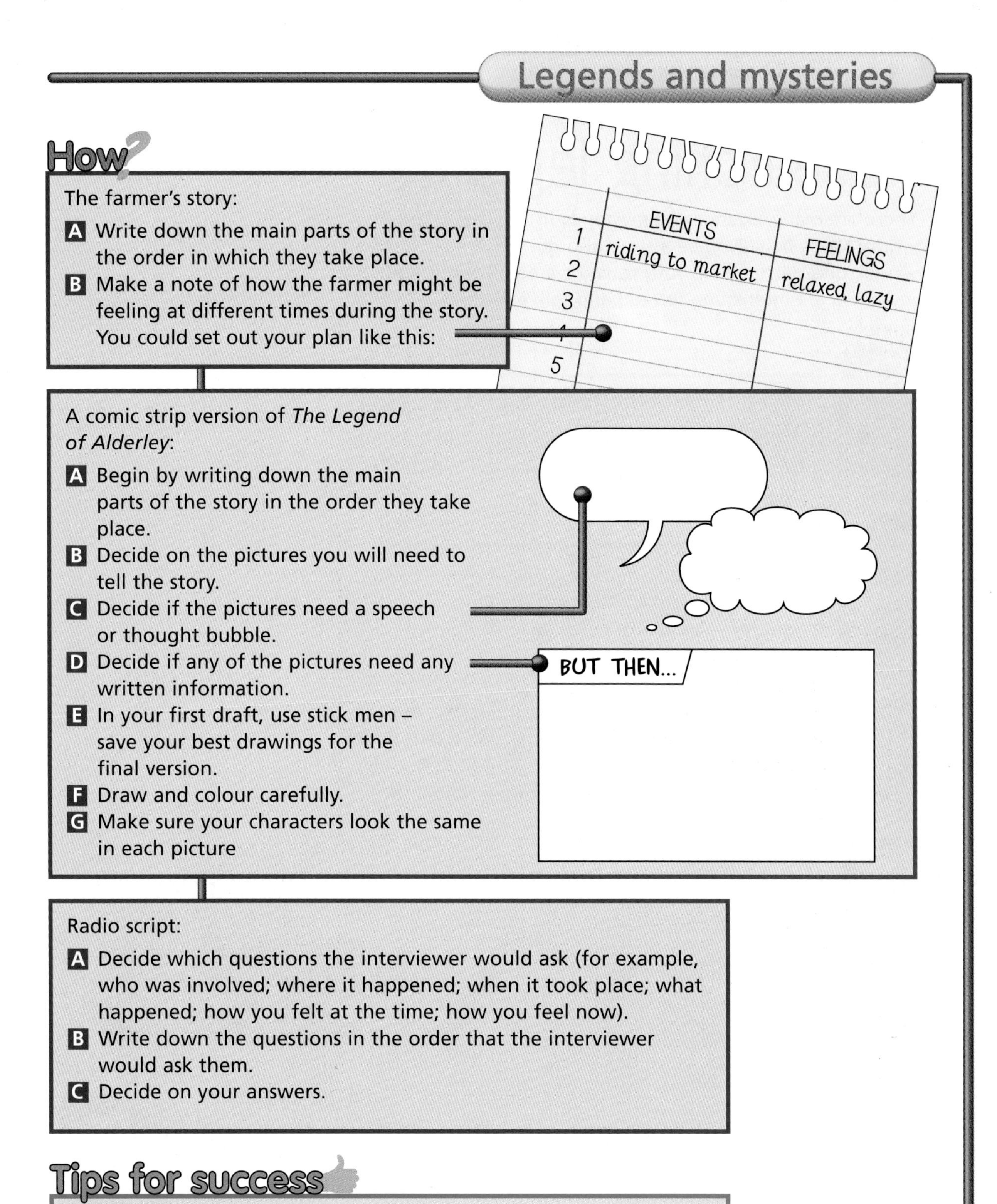

The farmer's story:

A Write down the main parts of the story in the order in which they take place.

B Make a note of how the farmer might be feeling at different times during the story. You could set out your plan like this:

A comic strip version of *The Legend of Alderley*:

A Begin by writing down the main parts of the story in the order they take place.

B Decide on the pictures you will need to tell the story.

C Decide if the pictures need a speech or thought bubble.

D Decide if any of the pictures need any written information.

E In your first draft, use stick men – save your best drawings for the final version.

F Draw and colour carefully.

G Make sure your characters look the same in each picture

Radio script:

A Decide which questions the interviewer would ask (for example, who was involved; where it happened; when it took place; what happened; how you felt at the time; how you feel now).

B Write down the questions in the order that the interviewer would ask them.

C Decide on your answers.

Tips for success

- Write neatly.
- Choose to work on the legend or mystery that you enjoyed reading about the most.
- Re-read the story before you begin.
- Write a draft version of your work and correct any mistakes that you find before you present your finished work.
- Use a dictionary to check your spelling.
- Make sure you write in sentences.

Researching legends

There are many legends and mysteries from around the world. There may even be a story about a place near to your school, or a person from your town or area. Legends and mysteries are interesting to read and talk about.

Task

Find out as much as you can about one legend or mystery.

Make notes about your chosen subject.

How?

A Use the following questions to help you to make notes:
Where did the legend or mystery take place?
When did the legend or mystery take place?
Who is involved in the story?
What are the main events of the legend or mystery?

B Use your school or local library to find more information. Use CD-ROMs or books, including encyclopaedias, to help you.

C Think about any films or T.V. programmes that mention your chosen legend.

D Here are some ideas of mysteries or legends that you may want to research:
- Corn Circles.
- U.F.O.s.
- King Arthur.
- The Loch Ness Monster.
- Robin Hood.
- The Yeti.
- The Lost City of Atlantis.
- The Nazca Lines of Peru.

Tips for success

- Use the How? box to help you through the activity.
- Choose your legend or mystery with care.
- Talk about your choice with your teacher before you start writing.
- Write down only the most important details of the story.
- Write neatly.

Comparing and contrasting

Task

Work with at least one other person.

Compare your chosen legend or mystery with *The Legend of Alderley* or the Bermuda Triangle.

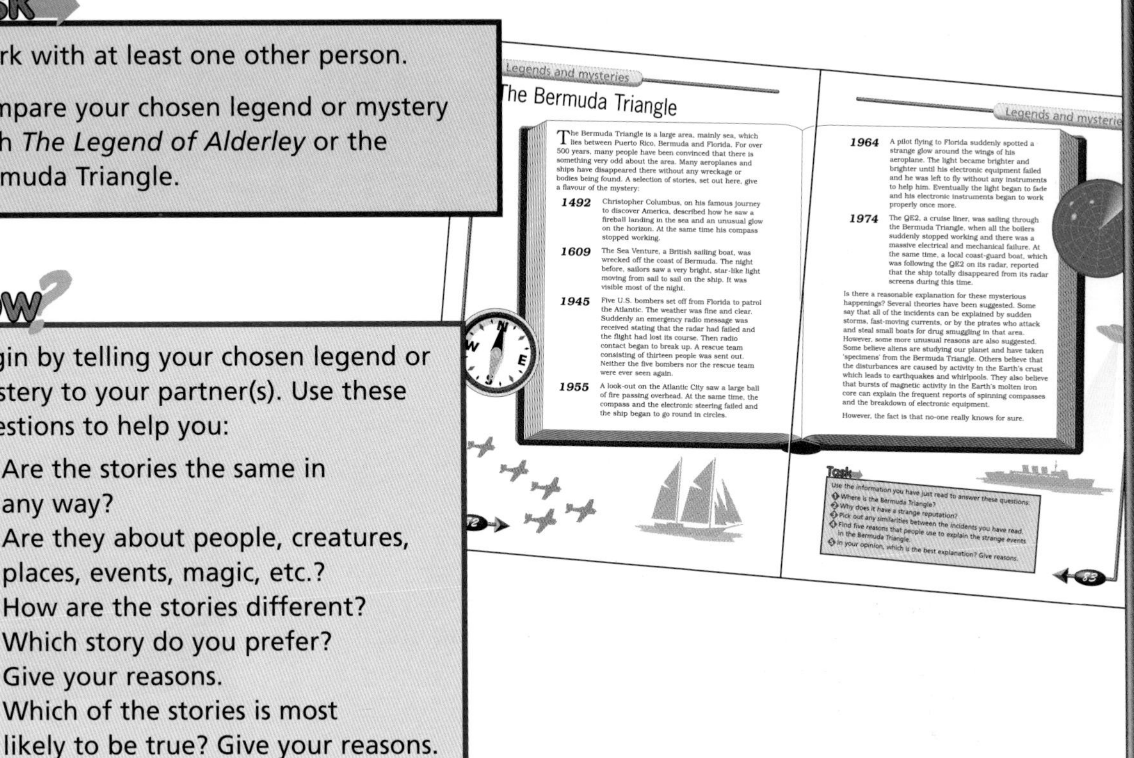

Legends and mysteries

The Bermuda Triangle

The Bermuda Triangle is a large area, mainly sea, which lies between Puerto Rico, Bermuda and Florida. For over 500 years, many people have been convinced that there is something very odd about the area. Many aeroplanes and ships have disappeared there without any wreckage or bodies being found. A selection of stories, set out here, give a flavour of the mystery:

1492 Christopher Columbus, on his famous journey to discover America, described how he saw a fireball landing in the sea and an unusual glow on the horizon. At the same time his compass stopped working.

1609 The Sea Venture, a British sailing boat, was wrecked off the coast of Bermuda. The night before, sailors saw a very bright, star-like light moving from sail to sail on the ship. It was visible most of the night.

1945 Five U.S. bombers set off from Florida to patrol the Atlantic. The weather was fine and clear. Suddenly an emergency radio message was received stating that the radar had failed and the flight had lost its course. Then radio contact began to break up. A rescue team consisting of thirteen people was sent out. Neither the five bombers nor the rescue team were ever seen again.

1955 A look-out on the Atlantic City saw a large ball of fire passing overhead. At the same time, the compass and the electronic steering failed and the ship began to go round in circles.

1964 A pilot flying to Florida suddenly spotted a strange glow around the wings of his aeroplane. The light became brighter and brighter until his electronic equipment failed and he was left to fly without any instruments to help him. Eventually the light began to fade and his electronic instruments began to work properly once more.

1974 The QE2, a cruise liner, was sailing through the Bermuda Triangle, when all the boilers suddenly stopped working and there was a massive electrical and mechanical failure. At the same time, a local coast-guard boat, which was following the QE2 on its radar, reported that the ship totally disappeared from its radar screens during this time.

Is there a reasonable explanation for these mysterious happenings? Several theories have been suggested. Some say that all of the incidents can be explained by sudden storms, fast-moving currents, or by the pirates who attack and steal small boats for drug smuggling in that area. However, some more unusual reasons are also suggested. Some believe aliens are studying our planet and have taken 'specimens' from the Bermuda Triangle. Others believe that the disturbances are caused by activity in the Earth's crust which leads to earthquakes and whirlpools. They also believe that bursts of magnetic activity in the Earth's molten iron core can explain the frequent reports of spinning compasses and the breakdown of electronic equipment.

However, the fact is that no-one really knows for sure.

Task

Use the information you have just read to answer these questions:

1. Where is the Bermuda Triangle?
2. Why does it have a strange reputation?
3. Pick out any similarities between the incidents you have read.
4. Find five reasons that people use to explain the strange events in the Bermuda Triangle.
5. In your opinion, which is the best explanation? Give reasons.

82 83

How?

Begin by telling your chosen legend or mystery to your partner(s). Use these questions to help you:

- **A** Are the stories the same in any way?
- **B** Are they about people, creatures, places, events, magic, etc.?
- **C** How are the stories different?
- **D** Which story do you prefer? Give your reasons.
- **E** Which of the stories is most likely to be true? Give your reasons.

Tips for success

- Make sure you understand the tasks.
- Making notes before the discussion may help you to remember the things you want to talk about.
- Use the How? box to help you through the activity.
- Speak clearly.
- Explain carefully.
- Listen to others.
- Take turns.

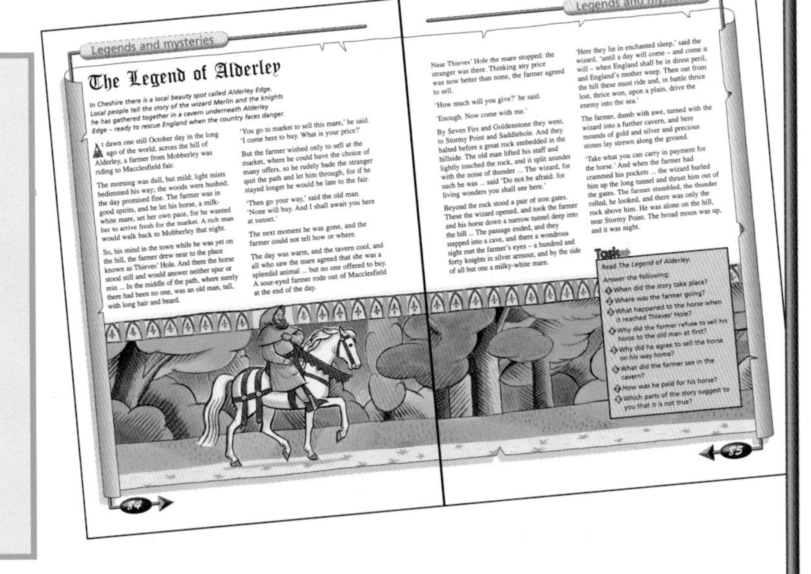

Legends and mysteries

The Legend of Alderley

In Cheshire there is a local beauty spot called Alderley Edge. Local people tell the story of the wizard Merlin and the knights he has gathered together in a cavern underneath Alderley Edge – ready to rescue England when the country faces danger.

At dawn one still October day in the long ago of the world, across the hill of Alderley, a farmer from Mobberley was riding to Macclesfield fair.

The morning was dull, but mild; light mists bedimmed his way; the woods were hushed; the day promised fine. The farmer was in good spirits, and he let his horse, a milk-white mare, set her own pace, for he wanted her to arrive fresh for the market. A rich man would walk back to Mobberley that night.

So, his mind in the town while he was yet on the hill, the farmer drew near to the place known as Thieves' Hole. And there the horse stood still and would answer neither spur or rein ... In the middle of the path, where surely there had been no one, was an old man, tall, with long hair and beard.

'You go to market to sell this mare,' he said. 'I come here to buy. What is your price?'

But the farmer wished only to sell at the market, where he could have the choice of many offers, so he rudely bade the stranger quit the path and let him through, for if he stayed longer he would be late to the fair.

'Then go your way,' said the old man. 'None will buy. And I shall await you here at sunset.'

The next moment he was gone, and the farmer could not tell how or where.

The day was warm, and the tavern cool, and all who saw the mare agreed that she was a splendid animal ... but no one offered to buy. A sour-eyed farmer rode out of Macclesfield at the end of the day.

Near Thieves' Hole the mare stopped: the stranger was there. Thinking any price was now better than none, the farmer agreed to sell.

'How much will you give?' he said.

'Enough. Now come with me.'

By Seven Firs and Goldenstone they went, to Stormy Point and Saddlebole. And they halted before a great rock embedded in the hillside. The old man lifted his staff and lightly touched the rock, and it split asunder with the noise of thunder ... The wizard, for such he was ... said 'Do not be afraid: for living wonders you shall see here.'

Beyond the rock stood a pair of iron gates. These the wizard opened, and took the farmer and his horse down a narrow tunnel deep into the hill ... The passage ended, and they stepped into a cave, and there a wondrous sight met the farmer's eyes – a hundred and forty knights in silver armour, and by the side of all but one a milky-white mare.

'Here they lie in enchanted sleep,' said the wizard, 'until a day will come – and come it will – when England shall be in direst peril, and England's mother weep. Then out from the hill these must ride and, in battle thrice lost, thrice won, upon a plain, drive the enemy into the sea.'

The farmer, dumb with awe, turned with the wizard into a further cavern, and here mounds of gold and silver and precious stones lay strewn along the ground.

'Take what you can carry in payment for the horse.' And when the farmer had crammed his pockets ... the wizard hurled him up the long tunnel and thrust him out of the gates. The farmer stumbled, the thunder rolled, he looked, and there was only the rock above him. He was alone on the hill, near Stormy Point. The broad moon was up, and it was night.

Task

Read The Legend of Alderley.

Answer the following:

1. When did the story take place?
2. Where was the farmer going?
3. What happened to the horse when it reached Thieves' Hole?
4. Why did the farmer refuse to sell his horse to the old man at first?
5. Why did he agree to sell the horse on his way home?
6. What did the farmer see in the cavern?
7. How was he paid for his horse?
8. Which parts of the story suggest to you that it is not true?

84 85

Drama

Objectives

In successfully completing this unit, you will:

1. Talk about the main parts of a play.
2. Talk and write about one character from a play.
3. Design and produce a theatre programme.
4. Write about an issue raised by the play.
5. Take part in a role-play.

Introduction

In this unit you will look at the play *An Inspector Calls*. You will then write about the character of Arthur Birling, and the issue of poverty raised in the play. You will also produce a theatre programme.

Task

Look at the pictures on the previous page.

Discuss what goes into a play.

How?

During your discussion, you might talk about:

A Where the action seems to be taking place.
B The information you gain from the characters' clothing.
C The expression on the characters' faces.
D Whether the picture gives you any ideas about what is happening in the play.

Tips for success

- Make sure you understand the tasks.
- Making notes before the discussion may help you to remember the things you want to talk about.
- Use the How? box to help you through the activity.
- Speak clearly.
- Explain carefully.
- Listen to others.
- Take turns.

Cardiff Roundhouse
presents
Murder in the Woods
Seat: DD9 £7.00
Upper Circle

Belfast Amateur Players
present
"My Wonderful Life"
Performance: Matinée
Seat Number: H4
Price: £6

Dundee Windmill Theatre
The Yellow Rose
Evening Performance
J15

Dundee Windmill Theatre
PRESENTS
The Yellow Rose
Evening Performance
Stalls
Seat No: J15
Ticket Price: £5.00

Researching your subject

Now that you have looked at the ingredients that make up a play, you are going to concentrate on *An Inspector Calls* and in particular on the character of Arthur Birling.

However, before you move on to look at him in detail, you are going to find out about some of the important issues he talks about at the beginning of the play.

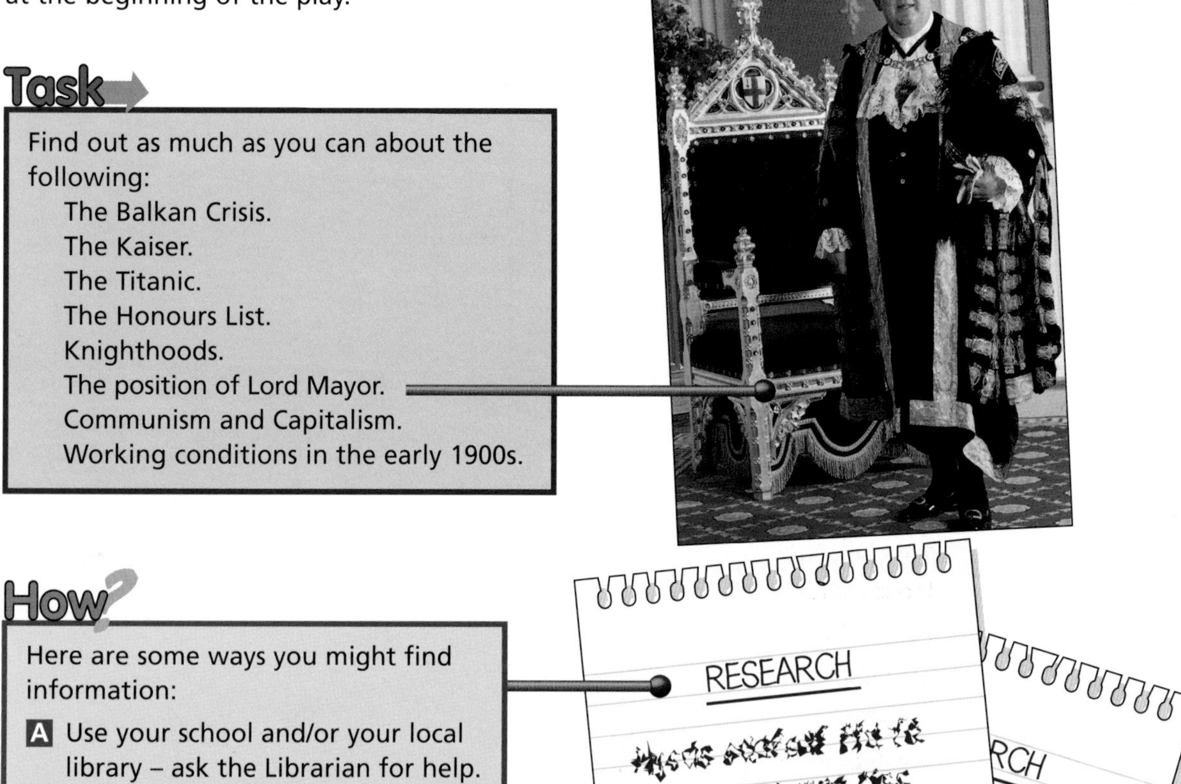

Task

Find out as much as you can about the following:

- The Balkan Crisis.
- The Kaiser.
- The Titanic.
- The Honours List.
- Knighthoods.
- The position of Lord Mayor.
- Communism and Capitalism.
- Working conditions in the early 1900s.

How?

Here are some ways you might find information:

A Use your school and/or your local library – ask the Librarian for help.

B Use an encyclopaedia, reference book, or CD-ROM.

C Ask your History teachers.

RESEARCH

Tips for success

- Make notes to help you remember the information you find.
- Work in groups and share out the research between the members of the group.

An Inspector Calls

Now look carefully at the following extract from the beginning of the play. It takes place at the end of a meal to celebrate the engagement of Arthur Birling's daughter, Sheila, to Gerald Croft.

ACT ONE

BIRLING I'm delighted about this engagement and I hope it won't be too long before you're married. And I want to say this. There's a good deal of silly talk about these days – but – and I speak as a hard-headed business man, who has to take risks and know what he's about – I say, you can ignore all this silly pessimistic talk. When you marry, you'll be marrying at a very good time. Yes, a very good time – and soon it'll be an even better time. Last month, just because the miners came out on strike, there was a lot of wild talk about possible labour trouble in the near future. Don't worry. We've passed the worst of it. We employers at last are coming together to see that our interests – and the interests of Capital – are properly protected. And we're in for a time of steadily increasing prosperity.

GERALD I believe you're right, sir.

Right, a scene from the 1997 Royal National Theatre's production of *An Inspector Calls*.

The play continues with Arthur Birling talking about how happy he is with life in general. In this part of the conversation we learn about:

- The kind of a person he is.
- What he believes about the country.
- His thoughts about world events.

ACT ONE

ERIC What about war?

BIRLING Glad you mentioned it, Eric. I'm coming to that. Just because the Kaiser makes a speech or two, or a few German officers have too much to drink and begin talking nonsense, you'll hear some people say that war's inevitable. And to that I say – fiddlesticks! The Germans don't want war. Nobody wants war, except some half-civilised folks in the Balkans. And why? There's too much at stake these days. Everything to lose and nothing to gain by war.

ERIC Yes, I know – but still –

BIRLING Just let me finish, Eric. You've a lot to learn yet. And I'm talking as a hard-headed practical man of business. And I say there isn't a chance of war. The world's developing so fast that it'll make war impossible. Look at the progress we're making. In a year or two we'll have aeroplanes that will be able to go anywhere. And look at the way the auto-mobile's making headway – bigger and faster all the time. And then ships. Why, a friend of mine went over this new liner last week – The Titanic – she sails next week – forty-six thousand eight hundred tons – New York in five days – and every luxury – and unsinkable, absolutely unsinkable...

Task

Write down the answers to these questions:

1. Why does Birling think it is a "good time" to get engaged?
2. How far do you agree with him? Base your answer on the information you found when doing your research.

How?

Read the extract very carefully.

Find any comments Birling makes about the subjects that you researched.

Now read on ...

Task

Read the extract carefully.

ACT ONE

BIRLING By the way, there's something I'd like to mention – in strict confidence – while we're by ourselves. I have an idea that your mother – Lady Croft – while she doesn't object to my girl – feels you might have done better for yourself socially – GERALD, *rather embarrassed, begins to murmur some dissent, but* BIRLING *checks him.* No, Gerald, that's all right. Don't blame her. She comes from an old country family – landed people and so forth – and so it's only natural. But what I wanted to say is – there's a fair chance that I might find my way into the next Honours List. Just a knighthood, of course.

GERALD Oh – I say – congratulations!

BIRLING Thanks. But it's a bit too early for that. So don't say anything. But I've had a hint or two. You see I was Lord Mayor here two years ago when Royalty visited us. And I've always been regarded as a sound, useful party man. So – well – I gather there's a very good chance of a knighthood – so long as we behave ourselves, don't get into the police court or start a scandal – eh? *(Laughs complacently.)*

NT Royal National Theatre

"one of the most intoxicating, theatrically imaginative experiences of the 1990s"

Evening Standard

JB Priestley's Classic Thriller

An Inspector Calls

Now talk with at least one other person about Birling's reasons for mentioning he was Lord Mayor and the possibility that he may receive a knighthood.

And finally ...

Task

Read the extract carefully.

ACT ONE

ERIC	Mother says we mustn't stay too long. But I don't think it matters. I left 'em talking about clothes again. You'd think a girl had never had any clothes before she gets married. Women are potty about 'em.
BIRLING	Yes, but you've got to remember, my boy, that clothes mean something quite different to a woman. Not just something to wear – and not only something to make 'em look prettier – but – well, a sort of sign or token of their self-respect.
GERALD	That's true.
ERIC	*(Eagerly.)* Yes, I remember – *(Checks himself.)*
BIRLING	Well, what do you remember?
ERIC	*(Confused.)* Nothing.
GERALD	*(Amused.)* Sounds a bit fishy to me.
BIRLING	*(Taking it in the same manner.)* Yes, you don't know what some of these boys get up to nowadays. More money to spend and time to spare than I had when I was Eric's age. They worked us hard in those days and kept us short of cash. Though even then – we broke out and had a bit of fun sometimes.
GERALD	I'll bet you did.
BIRLING	*(Solemnly.)* But this is the point. I don't want to lecture you two young fellows again. But what so many of you don't seem to understand now, when things are so much easier, is that a man has to make his own way – has to look after himself – and his family too, of course, when he has one – and so long as he does that, he won't come to much harm. But the way some of these cranks talk and write now, you'd think everybody has to look after everybody else, as if we're all mixed up together like bees in a hive – community and all that nonsense...

Task

Now write down the answers to the following questions:

1. What does Birling tell Eric and Gerald about how they should treat:
   a) their families;
   b) other people?
2. What does Birling think about women?
3. What kind of person does Birling seem to be? Base your answer on all that you have read so far, including your research.

Discussing Arthur Birling

So far, you have concentrated on parts of a speech by Arthur Birling from the early part of the play. You are now going to write about the sort of person Arthur Birling is using some additional comments made by himself and some of the other characters.

Task

Read the quotations.

Note down what they you tell you about the character of Arthur Birling.

Use your knowledge of the play to explain why.

How?

A Look at the words and phrases that follow. Use these to help you describe Birling: ruthless; only interested in himself and his family; narrow-minded; can't always accept the results of his actions; full of his own importance; hard to talk to; not a good listener.

B Set out your work in columns like this:

Quotation	What this tells us about Birling	Reason
I've got to cover this up ...	Ruthless	

Tips for success

- Look up any words that you do not understand.

Rich and poor

In this part of the unit, you are going to look at one of the issues which is raised in the play – poverty.

England at the time of the play (1900s) was a country where some people, like the Birlings, were very rich and others, like Eva Smith (who is discussed later in the play), were very poor. In the play we learn that Eva was so poor that she asked for a rise when she worked at Birling's and had to beg for charity when she was pregnant.

Poverty at the beginning of the 20th century was widespread. The poor would work very long hours, about 60 a week, for extremely low wages. Women, like Eva, would normally earn about half of what a man earnt. Poor families would often not be able to afford the basics, and certainly could not give pocket-money to their children, smoke or drink, or buy extra clothing 'for best'. They would not be able to take time off from work, even when they felt ill. If they did, they would not be paid and might even lose their jobs. Money had to be used to pay for food, rent and essential clothing. Housing was very poor and overcrowded. Sickness and ill-health were common. Many poor people died when they were very young.

Life for the rich was very different. Houses were big and well furnished and many families had servants. A nanny would look after the children and be responsible for their early education. Nannies also ensured that rich children were kept away from the poor. Their better diet and living conditions meant that the rich were generally much healthier than the poor. However, if they did fall ill, their families could afford to pay for a doctor, something that was well out of the reach of the poor, who had to rely on the service provided by the parish.

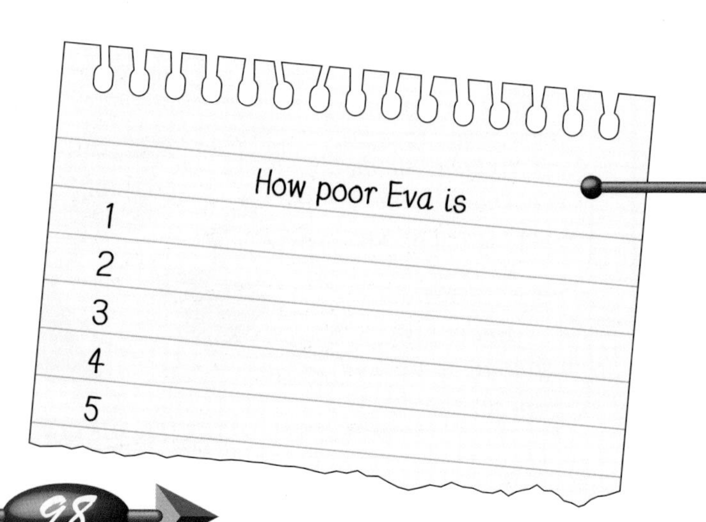

Task

Write down the answers to these questions:

1. List five things which the poor could not afford.
2. How did the poor spend their money?
3. What would happen if a poor worker was not able to go to work?
4. Describe how the rich lived.
5. Find five examples from the play to show how poor Eva was.
6. Find three examples from the play to show how rich Sheila was.
7. How do you feel about what you have read?

Produce your own programme

When you go to see a play, you will often get a programme, which tells you a little bit about the theatre, the play, and the actors in it.

Task

Produce a theatre programme for *An Inspector Calls*. You can use the names of a real theatre and actors, or make them up. The programme on page 95 might give you some ideas.

How?

You will need to include the following items in your programme:

- **A** An interesting cover design.
- **B** A cast list.
- **C** The actors' page (see page 100).
- **D** A brief outline of the play.
- **E** Some information about the characters.
- **F** A list of future events at the theatre.
- **G** Some advertisements.

The cover

Cover designs may use a photograph or illustration showing:

- A scene from the play.
- A major character.

Covers usually include:

- The name of the theatre.
- The title of the play.
- The name of the author.
- The date and time of the play.

Cast list

A cast list shows which actor is playing which part. It is usually set out like this:

The Crucible Theatre Trust Ltd presents

ONCE A CATHOLIC

a comedy by Mary O'Malley

Mother Peter	DOREEN KEOGH
Mother Basil	KATHLEEN MOFFATT
Mother Thomas Aquinas	DI LANGFORD
Mr. Emanuelli	TERRY MORTIMER
Father Mullarkey	TERENCE FRISBY
Mary Moony	FIONA McARTHUR
Mary McGinty	TINA JONES
Mary Gallagher	CLAIRE LEWIS
Mary O'Grady	KAREN DRURY
Mary Hennessy	AMANDA BELLAMY
Mary Murphy	BARBARA PEAK
Mary Flanagan	SABEL LANSDALE
Derek	GERRY HOLTON
Cuthbert	MARTYN HESFORD

The play is set in the Convent of Our Lady of Fatima – a Grammar School for Girls, and in and around the streets of Willesden and Harlesden, London NW10, from September 1956 to July 1957.

THERE WILL BE ONLY ONE INTERVAL

Directed by Michael Bogdanov
Assistant to the Director Paul Elkins
Designed by Rodney Ford
Lighting by Peter Barham
Sound by Caz Appleton

The actors' page

On this page you should give details about some of the other plays, films or T.V. programmes that the actors have appeared in. Here are some examples to look at:

An outline of the play

In this part of the programme you should set out to explain briefly the story of the play. You should include:

- An explanation of where and when the play takes place.
- Who is involved.
- A brief statement of what happens.

Future events

Most programmes include a list of plays, concerts and exhibitions that will take place in the near future in the theatre. Invent up to seven events for your chosen theatre. Vary the events. Include dates, times, and costs.

Advertisements

Many local companies will advertise in a local theatre's programme. You will be able to fill up the spaces on your pages with advertisements.

Tips for success

- Think carefully about the size and layout of your programme.
- Think carefully about the actors you want to play the parts in the play.
- Make sure that the information that you give is clearly and neatly set out.
- Make sure that your finished programme is bright and attractive.

Leaham Globe Actors' Spotlight

Paul Belomey

Paul was born in Bristol and trained at the University of Birmingham and the Actors' Forum. He began his professional career at the Crucible Theatre. Since then he has appeared in a wide variety of roles, ranging from Macbeth to Charlie Chaplin! Other theatre roles include Mercutio in ROMEO AND JULIET, Jean in RHINOCEROS and the Tin Man in the WIZARD OF OZ. T.V. credits include CORONATION STREET, THE BILL, and MY FAMILY AND OTHER ANIMALS.

Julia Cook

Julia Cook is twelve years old and is in her first year at Leaham High School. She has lived nearly all her life in the town and, apart from some minor roles in her junior school annual plays, this is her first theatrical appearance.

And finally ...

One of the main issues in the play is the idea of taking responsibility for your actions. All of the Birlings and Gerald Croft have played a part in what happens to Eva Smith. Some of them, like Sheila, feel guilty about what they have done. Others do not.

Gerald Croft

Task

Role-play a conversation about Eva Smith's death between any two of the following characters:

Sheila.
Mrs Birling.
Eric.
Mr Birling.
Gerald.

Sheila

How?

A Think about how your chosen character feels about what has happened to Eva.
B Think about what your character has learned about:
Himself or herself.
The other character in your role play.
The rest of the characters in the play.
C Decide where and when your conversation will take place.
D Begin with the line: "Who do you blame for Eva Smith's death"?

LADY CROFT

Eric

Tips for success

- Plan your conversation before you start.
- Make sure that you stay in character.
- Try to make the conversation as realistic as possible.

Arthur Birling

Leisure

Objectives

In successfully completing this unit, you will:

1. Choose and describe two leisure activities.
2. Carry out a survey of leisure activities and record the results.
3. Find out and write about a local leisure facility.
4. Find out and write about a leisure activity that you have not previously tried.

Introduction

Task

Look at the pictures on the previous page.

Discuss the variety of leisure activities they show.

How?

During your discussion, you might talk about:

A Which activities you have already tried.
B Which ones you would like to try – give reasons.
C Activities in which you are interested but are not shown.
D Activities that you know are available locally.
E What 'leisure' means to different people.

Tips for success

- Make sure you understand the tasks.
- Making notes before the discussion may help you to remember the things you want to talk about.
- Use the How? box to help you through the activity.
- Speak clearly.
- Explain carefully.
- Listen to others.
- Take turns.

Don't be a couch-potato! Whether you want to develop new skills, gain more qualifications, or simply meet people and enjoy your leisure time, the Borough of Newland has just the thing for you. Enrol today for a better tomorrow!

Surfing the Internet

Newland College of FE
Tuesdays 6 p.m. – 8 p.m.

Learn to surf the Net and create your own Website.

Ten sessions £30

Newland Amateur Dramatic Society

St Mary's Church Hall
Mondays and Fridays 7 p.m. – 10 p.m.

Join the gang for this year's production of *West Side Story*.

New members welcome

Subscription £2 per week

DIY

Newland High school
Wednesday 7 p.m. – 9.30 p.m.

Save yourself a fortune in repair bills. Under the guidance of our expert tutors' you can develop a range of useful skills.

Ten sessions £35

Model Railway Society

St Mary's Church Hall
Every evening after 6 p.m.

With 100 metres of track already constructed and landscaped, help to recreate the Tyne Valley's Steam-age rail system.

New members welcome.

Subscription £1.75

Line Dancing

Newland Community Centre
Mondays 7.30 p.m. – 10 p.m

Enjoy the fastest growing dance craze to hit this country since the 1960s. Buy a Stetson and mosey on down every Monday to meet cowboys and cowgirls of all ages.

Entrance fee £3 per session

Art Class

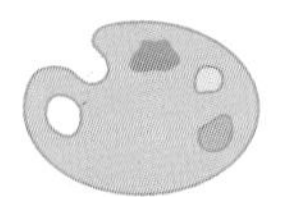

Newland College of FE
Thursday 6.30 p.m. – 9 p.m.

Whether your style is Rembrant or Picasso, Da Vinci or Hockney, beginner or expert, we can help you discover and develop your talent.

Express yourself in drawing, painting, clay or ceramics.

16 weeks £30

Are you looking to improve your qualifications?

Courses are available in a wide range of subjects at both GCSE and GNVQ levels. This is the opportunity you have been waiting for if you need to gain recognition of your abilities to advance your career prospects. Visit either:

Newland High School or
Newland College of FE

where further information and course details will be explained to you.

Courses include:

GCSEs	GNVQs
English	*Tourism*
English Literature	*Catering*
Mathematics	*Construction*
Science	
Modern Languages	
Information Technology	

Newland Sports Centre

The Centre caters for all ages and types of activity. Our expert tutors and coaches are on-hand to meet your needs. Beginner or experienced sportsperson, we have just what you are looking for. Choose from our extensive list:

5-a-side football	*Badminton*
Scuba diving	*Martial arts*
In-line skating	*Roller hockey*
Keep fit	*Squash*
Table tennis	*Weight-training*

Details of courses available from our reception.

Flower Arranging for Beginners

St Mary's Church Hall
Wednesday 6 p.m. – 8 p.m.

Learn how to make the most of fresh flowers to beautify your home.

8 weeks £15

Parenting Skills

Newland High school
Monday 6.30 p.m. – 8 p.m.

Being a parent is one job we are rarely prepared for. Under the guidance of a nurse and health visitor, you can prepare for the patter of tiny feet or learn to deal with the joys and problems of parenthood.

Ten sessions £30

Task

Look at the What's on Guide on pages 104 and 105.

Choose two leisure activities.

Write about each of them as fully as you can.

How?

You should think about:

A Where the activity takes place.
B When the activity takes place.
C What sort of equipment you will need.
D What the activity involves.
E What sort of person the activity appeals to.

Look at the Research box below.

Tips for success

- Make sure you read the What's on Guide very carefully.
- Use the How? box to help you through the activity.
- Write neatly in sentences.
- Use paragraphs.
- Check spellings and punctuation carefully.
- Read your work through and make any necessary changes or corrections before presenting your work.

Research

You could make your descriptions much more detailed and entertaining if you found out more about your chosen activities. You could:

Talk to someone who does the activity.
Use your school/local library.
Use a CD-ROM, if available.

This graph shows the popularity of various leisure activities in Newland.

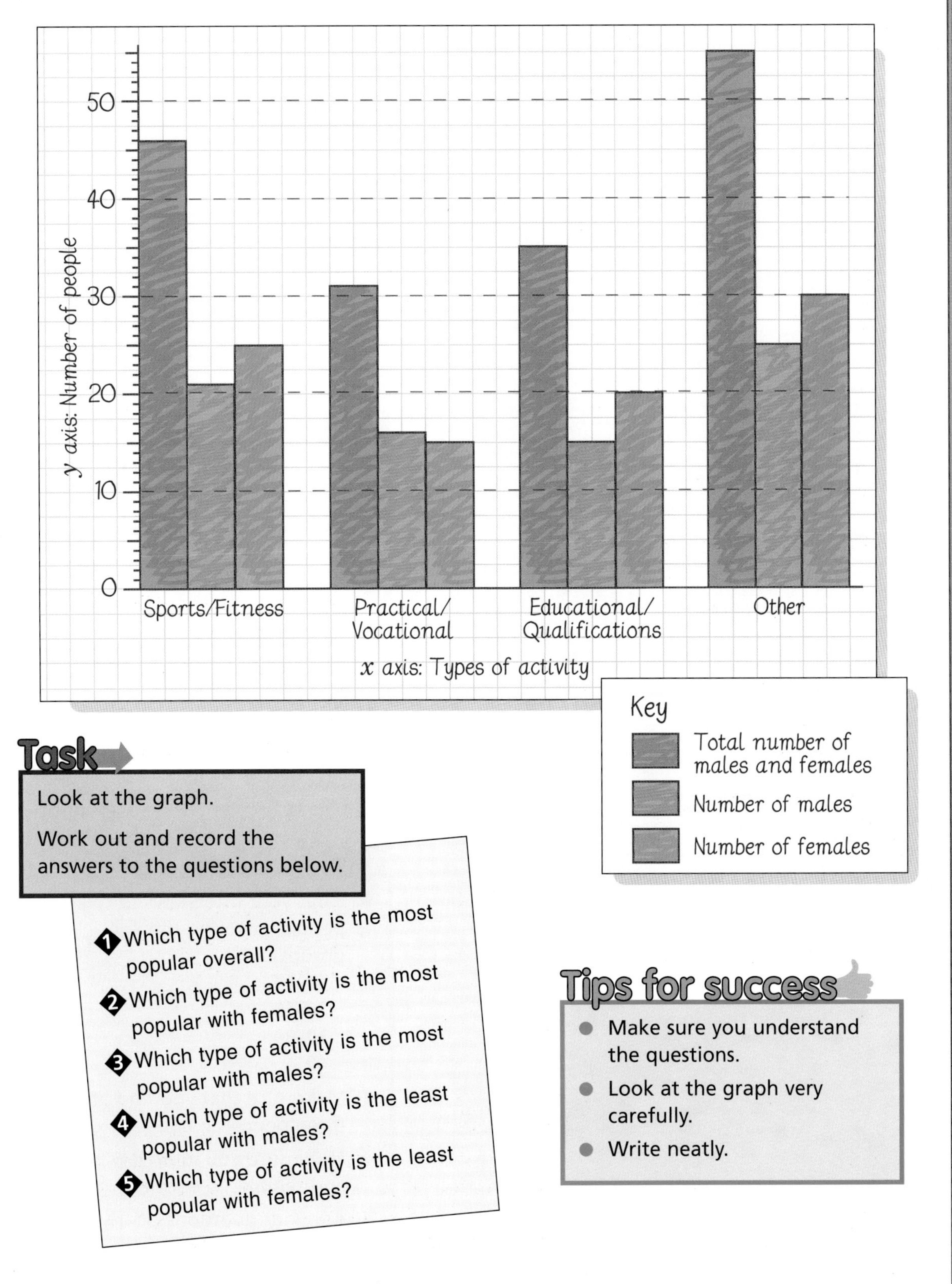

Task

Look at the graph.

Work out and record the answers to the questions below.

1. Which type of activity is the most popular overall?
2. Which type of activity is the most popular with females?
3. Which type of activity is the most popular with males?
4. Which type of activity is the least popular with males?
5. Which type of activity is the least popular with females?

Tips for success

- Make sure you understand the questions.
- Look at the graph very carefully.
- Write neatly.

Designing a leisure survey

Having looked at the information contained in the graph on leisure activities in Newland, you are now going to carry out a survey in **your** local area.

Task

Design a questionnaire to gather information about how people in your area spend their leisure time.

How?

You will need to find out the following:

A The ages of the people involved in the activities.
B The sort of person being interviewed (for example, male or female.)
C The favourite activities of each person.
D The time spent on each activity.

Tips for success

- Limit your interviews to twelve people, covering the age groups:
  14–19
  20–29
  30–39
  40+
- Make sure that you find at least three people in each age group.
- Make sure you interview males and females in each age group.
- Ask your questions clearly.
- Record the answers accurately.

Your turn

Task

Share your results with others in your class to help you to make a graph, similar to the one for Newland shown on page 107.

How?

A You need to ask questions that will help you to find out the total numbers of people involved in:
- Sports/Fitness
- Practical/Vocational
- Educational/Qualifications
- Other.

B Plot a simple bar chart to show the results.

Tips for success

- Look again at the graph on page 107.
- Make sure that you have enough space for each bar in your chart.
- Label the x axis Types of activity.
- Label the y axis Numbers of people.
- Use colours to represent each activity.

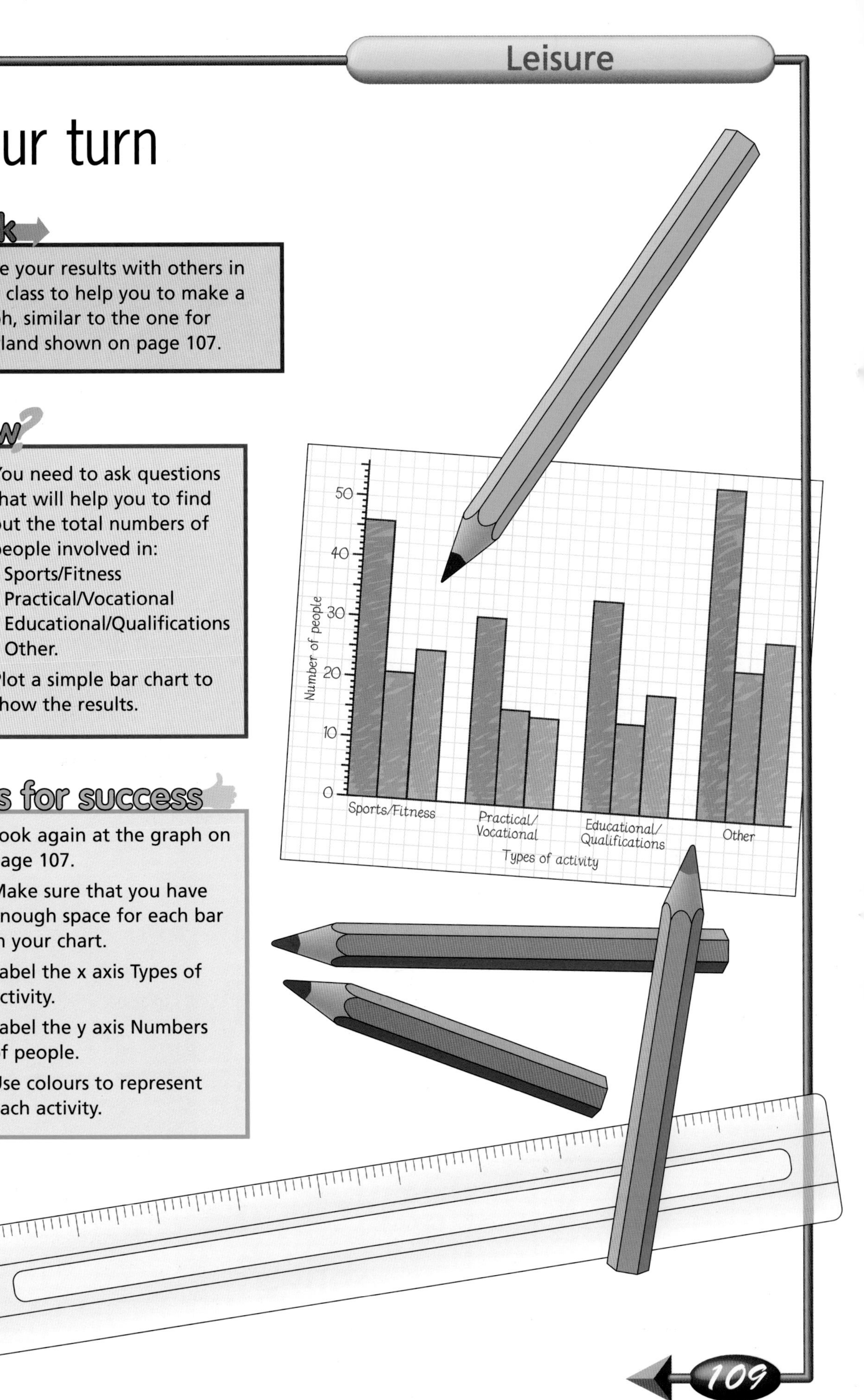

Local leisure

Task

Find out and write about at least one local leisure venue.

How?

- **A** Visit a local leisure venue.
- **B** Look at what is available.
- **C** Collect any suitable information, such as leaflets.
- **D** Record your information about the venue using the following headings:
  - Name of venue
  - Address
  - Telephone/fax number
  - Facilities available
  - Activities available
  - Opening times

Tips for success

- Make sure you understand the task.
- Making notes may help you to remember the things you need to write about.
- Use the How? box to help you through the activity.
- Write neatly.
- Use blue or black ink.

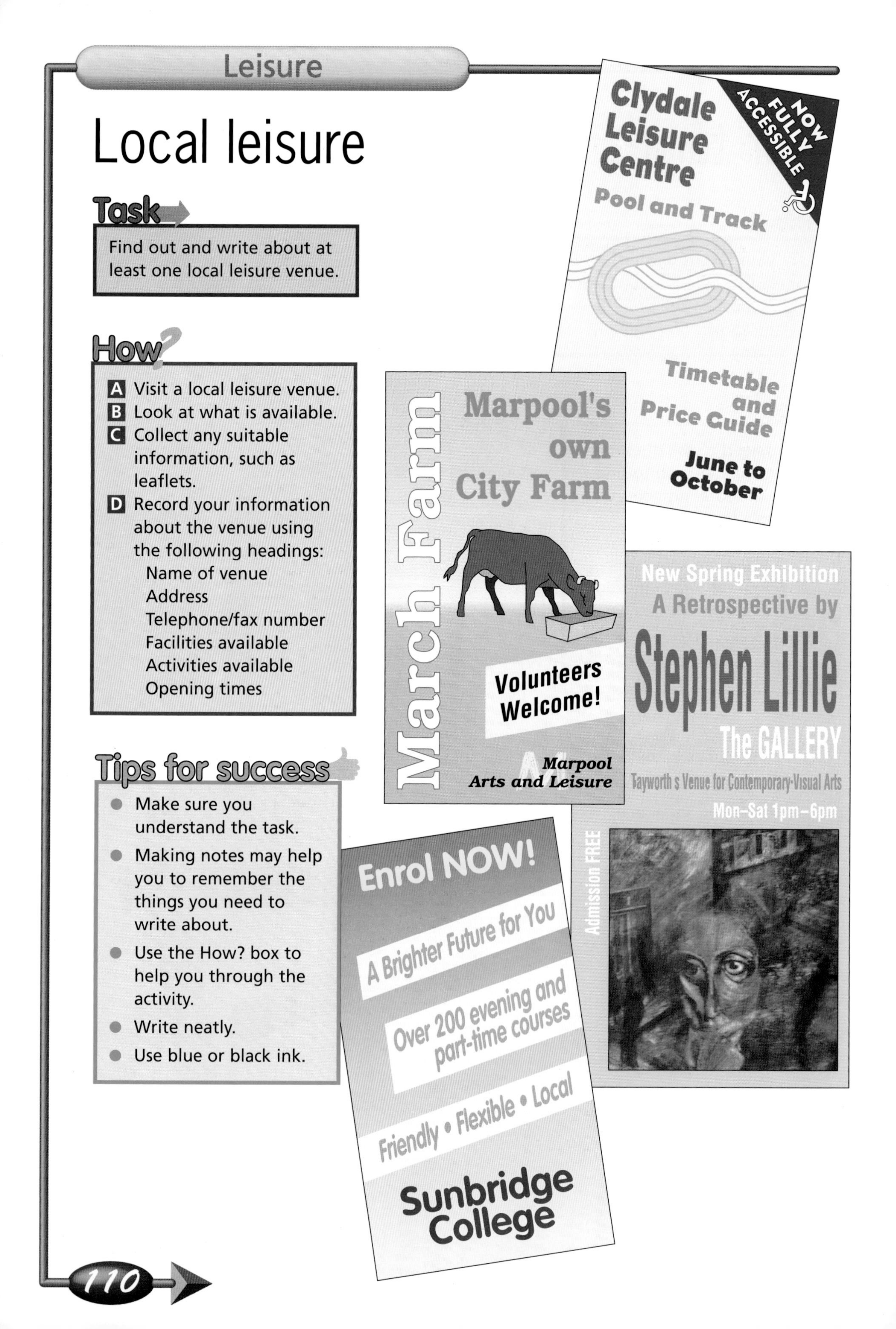

... And finally

Task

Find out about and write about an activity that you have not yet tried.

How?

A Look again at the What's on Guide to help you to choose an activity. (You might want to choose something which is not listed.)

B Find out about the leisure activity that interests you most. Use text books, CD-ROMs, leaflets and encyclopaedias to help you.

C You might talk to someone who does the activity.

D Find out about:

Where it takes place in your area.
The equipment needed.
When it takes place.
How the activity is carried out (for example, the rules).
How much it costs to take part.

Tips for success

- Arrange your information using headings.
- Draw diagrams if necessary.
- Write neatly in sentences.
- Use a dictionary to check spellings.
- Read your work carefully and make any necessary changes or corrections before presenting your final version.

Where	Equipment	When	Rules	Cost

Acknowledgements

The following publishers, authors and agents are thanked for permission to reproduce extracts and copyright material:

Tomato Sauce, published by Collins Educational, text © Brian Morse, illustrations © Mike Brownlow; *The Wasteland* by Alan Paton, from *Debbie Go Home*, published by Jonathan Cape; *My Brother* by Philip Campbell; *But You Didn't* by Merrill Glass, from *Discovering Poetry*, ed. Denise Scott, published by Heinemann; *I didn't think I had the power to leave the girls,* from *The Express,* 12th February 2000; *Geri: Leaving was like a marriage break-up,* from *The Sun*, 12th February 2000; *Drivers Call for Road Rage Laws*, *Ringo's Home is Starr Attraction, Two Killed in Blaze Horror, Tape Books all the Rage*, 5th May 1997; *Exclusive* by Bill Daniels from The *Evening Chronicle* 24th May 1997; *Man Charged With Abduction, Lanning on the Box*, from The *People*, 4th May 1997; *The Legend of Alderley*, from *The Weirdstone of Brisingamen* by Alan Garner, first published in 1960 by William Collins, © Alan Garner 1960; Extracts from *An Inspector Calls*, by J.B. Priestly, reprinted by permission of The Peters Fraser & Dunlop Group Limited on behalf of J.B. Priestly.

Photographs

The publishers would like to thank the following for permission to reproduce photographs (the page number is printed in bold and followed, where necessary, by t-top, b-bottom, l-left, r-right, m-middle):

4tl Madame Tussaud's; **4br** F.P.G. © Stephen Simpson/ Telegraph Colour Library; **4tr**, **4bl** V.C.L./Telegraph Colour Library; **5tr** Mark Stenning/Telegraph Colour Library; **5br** N. Daly/Telegraph Colour Library; **6** Mr Paul Von Stroheim/ Telegraph Colour Library; **7tr** Bavaria-Bildagentur/ Telegraph Colour Library; **7br** Yves Gellie/ Icone/Colorific!; **9** Logos reproduced with kind permission of The Commonwealth Experience, Madame Tussaud's, The London Planetarium, The London Dungeon, The Tower Bridge Experience; **10** Food Features; **11br** A. Zeplin/Telegraph Colour Library; **11m** V.C.L./Telegraph Colour Library; **11tr** Nick Wright/ Telegraph Colour Library; **12b** Martine Maouch/Tony Stone Worldwide; **12t** Phil Degginger/Tony Stone Worldwide; **14, 15, 46, 47** Reproduced courtesy of Harper Collins Publishers; **25** Peter Cade/Tony Stone Worldwide; **27, 45** J.P. Fruchet/Telegraph Colour Library; **28tr** © The Metropolitan Police Service; **28tl** Andrew Hay/R.S.P.B. Images; **28br**, F.P.G. © J. Cummins/Telegraph Colour Library; **28bl** Michael Rosenfeld/Tony Stone Worldwide; **29** National Dairy Council © 1987; **33** J. Price/Telegraph Colour Library; **34, 35** F.P.G. © A. Tilley/Telegraph Colour Library; **37, 78, 79** With kind permission of the Health Education Authority; **38** Andy Sacks/Tony Stone Worldwide; **42, 105** Masterfile/ Telegraph Colour Library; **53** Kevin Horan/Tony Stone Worldwide; **58, 80br** Hulton Getty; **59** Spencer Rowell/Telegraph Colour Library; **60** First pages reproduced by kind permission of the *Glasgow Evening Times*, Scottish Media Newspapers Ltd., The *Jewish Chronicle*, The *European*, The Mirror Group Newspapers; **62, 64, 65** PA News; **67, 70** Revlon International Corporation; **69, 70** Creative Fragrances; **77** Photo of David Lanning by kind permission of The *People*; **80tr** David Parker/ Science Photo Library; **80tl** F.P.G. © JF-MJC/Telegraph Colour Library; **80bl, 81** The Charles Walker Collection; **86** Diaouest/Telegraph Colour Library; **88** A.Gragera, Latin Stock/Science Photo Library; **90tr** Ben Elton's *Popcorn*, at the Apollo Theatre Shaftsbury Avenue, courtesy of Cameron Duncan Press & P.R.; **90bl** Chichester Festival Theatre's production of *Lady Windermere's Fan*, with Stephanie Beacham as Siri O'Neal, courtesy of the Chichester Festival Theatre's Press Office; **90tl** *King Lear*, with Kathryn Hunter as Lear and Robert Vaughan as Gloucester, courtesy of the Young Vic Theatre and KP Productions, photographer Stephen Vaughan; **90bl** *Smokey Joe's Cafe*, at the Prince of Wales Theatre, courtesy of the Turnstyle Group Limited, photographer Hugo Glendinning; **92** Alderman Sir Roger Cork, Lord Mayor of London, courtesy of the Public Relations Office, Corporation of London; **90, 95** The Royal National Theatre production of *An Inspector Calls*, at the Garrick Theatre, courtesy of McCabes; **100** Antonio Mo/Telegraph Colour Library; **102tr** Back Up; **102br** Stewart Cohen/Tony Stone Worldwide; 102tl Karen Mostavitz/Tony Stone Worldwide; **102bl** F.P.G. © C.J. Turner/Telegraph Colour Library; **108** All England Netball Association; **110** Stephen Lillie.

Every effort has been made to contact owners of copyright material but if any have been inadvertently overlooked the publishers will be pleased to make the necessary arrangements at the first opportunity.

Published by Collins Educational

An imprint of HarperCollins*Publishers* Ltd
77–85 Fulham Palace Road
London W6 8JB

First published 1997

ISBN 000 322 150 4

Malcolm White and Malcolm Seccombe assert the moral right to be identified as the authors of this work.

British Library Cataloguing in Publication Data.
A catalogue record for this book is available from the British Library.

Commissioned by Domenica de Rosa

Edited by Helen Clark, Paula Hammond

Cover design by Andrew Jones

Design by Ken Vail Graphic Design, Cambridge

Picture research by Katie Anderson, Paula Hammond

Production by Susan Cashin

Printed and bound by Printing Express, Hong Kong

Illustrations

Gerry Ball and Sam Thompson (Eikon Ltd), Ross (Archer Art), Graeme Morris (Ken Vail Graphic Design).

Reprinted 1998, 2001

With revisions 2000

www.CollinsEducation.com
On-line support for schools and colleges